Erasing The Guilt

Play An Active Role In Your Child's Education No Matter How Busy You Are

By Nancy S. Haug., M.S. and
Nancy D. Wright M.S., M.F.C.C.

THE CAREER PRESS
180 FIFTH AVE.
PO BOX 34
HAWTHORNE, NJ 07507
1-800-CAREER-1
201-427-0229 (OUTSIDE U.S.)
FAX: 201-427-2037

ERASING THE GUILT
Play an Active Role in your Child's Education
No Matter How Busy You Are
ISBN 1-56414-001-6, $10.95

Copies of this book may be ordered by mail or phone directly from the publisher. To order by mail, please include price as noted above, $2.50 handling per order, plus $1.00 for each book ordered. (New Jersey residents please add 7% sales tax.) Send to: The Career Press Inc., 180 Fifth Avenue., PO Box 34, Hawthorne, NJ 07507.

Or call Toll-Free 1-800-CAREER-1 to order using your VISA or Mastercard or for further information on all titles published or distributed by Career Press.

About The Authors

Nancy Wright
and
Nancy Haug

Nancy Haug holds a Master of Science degree in School Management and Administration. She taught at the elementary and junior high school levels for nine years. She has written articles on education and parenting that have appeared in a variety of publications, including *American Baby* and *Middle School Journal*. Nancy and her husband are the parents of four children, all under age 7.

Nancy Wright is a licensed Marriage, Family and Child Counselor with a Master of Science degree in Counseling. In addition to running a busy private practice, she leads seminars on topics ranging from stress management to infertility, and has appeared on *"The Oprah Winfrey Show."* Nancy and her husband have an 8-year-old son.

For information regarding professional speaking or services, call Nancy Wright at (714) 492-5636

Dedication

To J.D., who teaches me what's important in life.

And to Al, who always makes me smile.

To Claudio, Sarah, Eric, Brady, Brian and Mom for your love and support.

Table of Contents

Erasing The Guilt

Part Two: Time for School

Part Three: The After-school Hours

Introduction

Erasing The Guilt

> You bear a responsibility to participate actively in your child's education. You should encourage more diligent study and discourage satisfaction with mediocrity and the attitude that says 'let it slide'; monitor your child's study, encourage good study habits; encourage your child to take more demanding rather than less demanding courses; nurture your child's curiosity, creativity, and confidence; and be an *active participant in the work of the schools."*
>
> — the National Commission on Excellence in Education

Who would argue with that? We all agree. We all *want* to do more. We all want to spend more time and effort helping our children reach their potential. And if recent magazine and newspaper articles are to be believed, there is an inherent conviction that in order for your child to be successful, you *must* take an active role in the educational process.

Unfortunately, for all too many busy parents across the nation, such demands for greater parental involvement are not clarion calls to action. They simply generate an overwhelming sense of guilt—*because most parents don't feel they* have *the time to do more, even if they want to.*

We wholeheartedly agree that parental involvement is a key factor in a child's success in school. We do *not* feel, however, that parents should spend 18 years feeling guilty about what they should have done in the past, should do in the future, and do not have *time* to do today.

New parents receive an unexpected "gift" as their new "bundle of joy" enters the world—a nice big dose of guilt! Some carry it loosely with them at all times; others wear it like a noose around their necks. But no matter how you live and deal with it, the guilt is always there.

And it just *increases* when our children enter the school system, as we wonder how we can efficiently be involved in this critical process.

We began working on this book seated at a dining room table surrounded by five children. One was whining, two needed help putting together a Barbie hot dog stand, one was attempting to build a fort using a book shelf, and one had dirty diapers. While we reprimanded the whiner, put together the hot dog stand, kissed the bump on the head of the one who fell off the bookshelf, and changed the diaper of the baby on a dining room chair, we started laughing. How were *we* ever going to find the time to write this book...without feeling guilty about what else we weren't doing?

Both of us have many commitments and obligations, and both of us are committed to the education of our children. By following the advice of this book, we found that we effectively managed our *own* guilt and contributed to our children's education.

We are confident that you will, too!

Erasing the Guilt will finally give you the guilt-free guidelines to become actively involved in your children's education—providing schools and teachers with the support they need to educate your children and arming *you* with the tools to help them.

We are well aware that busy parents do not have time to read a complex, convoluted book. (If you did, you would not be feeling so harried and guilty, would you?) We therefore wrote concise chapters with a lot of pertinent, easy-to-implement ideas.

When you finish reading this book and applying the many tools it contains, *you* will feel a lot better and your *kids* a lot happier!

And you'll be confident that you are doing everything you can to help your children build a successful future. No matter *how* little time you can spare.

Part One

Laying The Groundwork

Chapter One

The Guilty Parent of the Nineties

"Parents set themselves up for guilt. From the moment children are born, we elevate them to the center of the universe. Schedules are readjusted, lifestyles change, sacrifices become a way of life. Nothing is going to get in the way of our children's happiness. Mother's guilt. Don't even think of leaving home without it."

— Erma Bombeck

As September approaches, Sandra Robinson, a researcher for a computer company, rushes around buying clothes, shoes, books and school supplies for her two children, Jeff, eight, and Kari, five. She has spent the last two weekends taking the kids shopping and arranging for after-school care.

Sandra's husband, Gary, is a salesman for a pharmaceutical company. Sandra and Gary have worked out a schedule of who will drop off and pick up the kids each day. There is a large calendar above the telephone in the kitchen. Soccer games, ballet classes, car pool days, and piano lessons are all marked in red ink.

Jeff, who will be starting the third grade, is an old hand at this annual ritual. Nevertheless, Sandra makes sure to discuss with him in what ways third grade will be harder than second. She stresses that he will have more homework. And warns him that she doesn't want any calls from the teacher saying that he's not turning in homework or completing assignments. Jeff's response is a typical, "Yeah, Mom. Don't worry."

Sandra takes extra time with Kari. They sit on the floor and play school. Kari wants to be the teacher. "Pay attention, please," she says, imitating her teacher. As Sandra sits quietly, Kari holds up pictures of different animals and asks her mother to name them. On purpose, Sandra makes a couple of mistakes and receives a stern look from teacher Kari. Next, they sing the alphabet song. Sandra gives Kari a hug, happy that her daughter is so excited about starting school.

Everyone wants your help...and time

During the first few weeks of school, Sandra and Gary, along with parents everywhere, begin receiving notices from school. There is an announcement for Back-to-school Night. On the bottom there is space for parents to sign up to volunteer in the classroom. Underneath the sign-up sheet, in bold letters, are the words **WE NEED YOUR HELP!**

For Sandra, Gary and parents across the nation, this is only the beginning. Most school principals send out letters detailing their philosophy and plans for the new school year. It is likely that the principal will stress the importance of *every* parent's active involvement in their children's education.

He may quote a study, such as a recent one from the National Committee for Citizens in Education: "Parent involvement in almost any form appears to produce measurable gains in student achievement...studies show that programs designed with a strong component of parental involvement produce students who perform better..."

Next comes the PTA drive: "Please enclose your check and join the PTA. Your child's future depends on it." Parents dutifully fill out the check and put it in the envelope. But wait...that's not all. The PTA wants you to attend the monthly meetings, and they are looking for volunteers. They need office and library helpers. They want help with the book fair, the "jog-a-thon," and the carnival. They need people to type, tutor, bake, clean up, and be on the organizing committees.

If you're not feeling guilty yet, Ann Lynch, National PTA President, stresses that your involvement is crucial because "your child will learn better, (his or) her school will be better, and (he or) she will get the best possible education."

Did *our* parents feel this guilty?

Has the educational system always demanded such involvement and participation? Have parents always felt so guilty? The answer to both questions is "No." Society has changed, the American family has changed, and the school system has changed.

In the 1950s, prominent educators decided that merely teaching reading, writing and arithmetic was not enough. Educators began to focus on the "total child," stressing not only academics but the student's psychological and physical well-being, as well.

This trend continues today—many schools now have classes on drug awareness, AIDS, sex education, self-esteem, and environmental and health issues. Teachers and the school system are being asked to do more than ever before.

At the same time, the nuclear family has undergone dramatic changes. *Newsweek* reports that 73 percent of mothers with school-age children work outside the home, and nearly one-fourth of all children under the age of 18 live with a single parent.

Homemaking mothers and breadwinning fathers are not the norm in the 1990s. Although roles are continually changing, in most families women still have the major responsibility for balancing family life and education. But men want to be more involved and take a more active role in this process.

These mothers and fathers are not raising their kids as they themselves were raised, and, as a result, they have no role models to emulate. They are being asked to be actively involved in their children's schooling while battling time constraints that their own parents did not experience. They feel overwhelmed by guilt as they struggle to balance home, school, and the demands of an increasingly changing world.

What *is* guilt?

"I feel guilty." No matter where you go—the market, a business meeting, a family gathering, or a cocktail party, if you stop and listen, sooner or later, you'll hear those words.

What is guilt? Technically, guilt occurs when we commit a breach of conduct or feel culpable. Realistically, we experience guilt when we think we should do something and don't or do something we later regret.

Tara has just returned home from her daughter's fourth-grade class where she helped the teacher with a special project. After leaving the classroom, she rushed around gathering newspapers for the school paper drive. Now she's off to her job at a local real estate company to meet a client. Tonight is her daughter's Back-to-school Night, but she has been looking forward to having dinner with a special friend.

At dinner that night she laments, "I feel terrible that I'm not at Stacy's Back-to-school Night. Her dad is there, but I feel guilty because *I* didn't go, too."

"Didn't you just spend some time in her classroom this morning?" asks her friend.

"Yes, but..."

"But nothing. Can't you relax for one evening without feeling guilty?"

"I guess not," Tara answers.

"Mom!" screams John.

"Finish your homework," answers Barbara, John's mother.

"I can't."

"What do you mean 'you can't?'"

"I don't understand it."

"Okay, bring it down and I'll help you. What don't you understand?"

"The whole thing!"

Twenty minutes later, Barbara and John have finished the assignment—that is, Barbara figured out the answers and John wrote them down. As Barbara begins dinner, she feels guilty because she actually *did* John's homework, rather than monitoring his efforts and giving selective help.

These two parents are suffering from *avoidable* guilt. In the following chapters, you will discover how to "erase" this unnecessary guilt.

Inescapable guilt

Although this book is entitled ***Erasing the Guilt,*** it is impossible to erase *all* guilt. In fact, an appropriate amount of guilt can be a constructive motivator. Guilt is an emotional response, not unlike happiness, sadness, embarrassment, anger and frustration. The ability to feel and express these emotions is part of what makes us human.

A father is on the phone while his child plays in front of the house. At the sound of screeching brakes, he drops the phone and rushes out the front door to find that a car has narrowly missed his daughter. His relief is palpable. So is his guilt. This is *inescapable guilt* because it is a normal human response.

Sometimes guilt becomes excessive, however, and we tell ourselves we should have done something that *realistically we could not have done.* This is *avoidable guilt* which can (and should) be eliminated.

The benefits of involvement

The word "involvement" inevitably suggests the concept of *time.* For busy parents, therefore, hearing the "I" word is the signal to run as fast as they can in the opposite direction.

"I don't know how Sue does it. She has four kids, and she always seems to know what's going on at school. She works part-time, and her kids are always well-behaved. I only have three kids, and I feel guilty that I don't seem to find the time to participate at school. I know school is important, yet this morning I was running so late that my kids missed the bus, and my oldest son hadn't even done his homework. I wish I could attend the PTA meetings, but I'm afraid they'll want me to do too much. I don't have enough time as it is."

Parents want to be active in educating their children. Administrators, teachers, and students all want parental involvement. No one, however, wants parents to become stressed, burned out and guilt ridden in the process. Even though that is usually exactly what occurs.

The first step in achieving guilt-free involvement is understanding why it is so crucial. Below you will find the benefits of school involvement to four groups: the child, the parents, the teacher and the school. In future chapters, you will learn specific ways to be involved in a time-efficient manner, minimizing your guilt while benefitting all concerned.

Benefits for the Child

1. Higher odds of success
2. Closer relationship with parent(s)
3. More willingness to participate
4. Better rapport with teacher
5. More secure regarding school

Benefits for Parents

1. Reduced guilt
2. Closer relationship with children
3. Better communication with teacher
4. Knowledge of child's social network
5. Awareness of child's progress

Benefits for Teachers

1. Morale and motivation better
2. Decreased workload
3. One-on-one work possible
4. Parent communication better
5. Better academic follow-through

Benefits for the School

1. Parents crucial to fundraisers
2. Community involvement better
3. Special events possible
4. Better attendance-higher funding
5. Enhances school-wide performance

Time pressure

The clock is ticking. Your children need to get up, dressed and off to school on time. You need to get breakfast on the table and lunches packed. You must arrive at work on time, complete projects, meet deadlines. You want to organize after-school activities, make sure groceries are bought, banking done, clothes cleaned, dinner cooked, homework completed, stories read...and, oh yes, you want to volunteer at school.

Sound familiar?

Thousands of parents repeat such a routine day after day. The pressures busy parents encounter are never-ending.

As is the feeling that there simply is *never* enough time. Einstein hadn't a clue how relative time *really* is—it's *always* in relatively short supply!

Now we have an extra added pressure. Schools and teachers are telling us, "In your *spare* time, we need your help." And parents are responding, "*What* spare time?"

The following chart offers an example of how a busy person's time is distributed throughout the day. Fill in the third column to see the amount of extra time *you* have available on an average day.

Time Distribution

Task	Person Working Full-Time (Hrs.)	Mother of Three (Hrs.)	Your Schedule (Hrs.)
Sleeping	7-1/2	7	____
Eating	1-1/2	1-1/2	____
Meal Preparation	1	2-1/2	____
Working	8	0	____
Personal Hygiene	1/2	1	____
Laundry	1/2	1-1/2	____
Household Chores	1	3	____
Errands	1	2	____
Personal	1/2	1	____
Other	1/2	1	
TOTAL	**22**	**20-1/2**	____
Time Left in a 24-hour Day	**2**	**3-1/2**	____

Chapter Two

Structure Saves Time

"Hey Eric! Come outside and go skateboarding with me!"

"I can't, Jake," says Eric, leaning out his bedroom window. "It's almost dark and I have to get my homework and chores done."

"Dark? Are you crazy? There's still light, and when the street lights go on, it'll be even brighter. C'mon, Eric, we can go down to the store. I've got money for gum."

"Nah, my mom's making dinner and she just told me to take a shower. Maybe tomorrow after school."

"Wow, Eric, your mom is really strict. You're eight years old and it's only six o'clock. Why can't you do that stuff later? It's early."

"I just can't, Jake. And anyway, my dad's reading me this great story and if I get into trouble, he won't finish it."

"You never get to do anything."

"It's not so bad. My mom and dad are just a little strange."

"Yeah, I guess so. Well, I gotta go, Eric.

"Bye, Jake."

Structure is the manner in which parts are organized to form a whole. Your child's day is composed of sleeping, eating, time at home, and time at school. If a similar level of structure exists at home and school, it becomes easier for your child to step in and out of his or her two worlds.

The amount of structure present in the school environment is a product of the large number of students that must be organized. An elementary school with an enrollment of 600, a teaching staff of 21, and an administrative staff of two could not possibly maintain order and productivity if each teacher adhered to his or her own timetable and agenda. State education codes determine how many minutes must be devoted to each area of instruction during an average day. The site administrator molds these requirements into a logical schedule, and district electricians activate the bell system. Thus your child's school day is structured into blocks of time, punctuated by breaks for food and play.

Within this established framework, the classroom teacher fits his or her curriculum. Though this series of required studies is determined at the state and local levels, each teacher's personality comes into play as the information is conveyed to the students.

One fifth-grade teacher may be highly structured and a strict disciplinarian. Her students raise their hands to sharpen their pencils and move about the school in a quiet line. In the next room, another fifth-grade teacher may have an informal approach. His students move about the room freely and participate in a variety of group projects.

Even given these radical differences in teaching style, both classes of fifth graders will follow similar time schedules and learn similar information. They will be expected to do their work quietly and complete it on time. Those who demonstrate the responsibility and self-control needed to function within the structure of the school day will most likely meet with success.

The teachers described here both provided structure, yet each colored it with his or her own distinctive flair. The same is true for parents at home. A registered nurse, comfortable with the type of structure she is accustomed to at work, may choose to have her children on a rather strict time schedule. Her neighbor, a self-employed architect with a casual work style, may abhor time constraints, yet provide structure in the form of an organized living space.

The following sections provide suggestions for structure in five different areas of home life—home organization, home responsibilities, consistent limits, and the structure of eating and sleeping.

Different options are presented so that parents may choose the ones that are consistent with their own personalities. Added structure has several benefits. A structured home life makes a child more secure and successful at school. In addition, structure helps parents save time and alleviate guilt.

Home organization

What we say

> "Your room is a mess! I see parts from games we don't even own anymore. Clean it up now!"
>
> "That dress is much too small to wear to school. It shouldn't even be in your drawer."

Guilty thoughts we think

"I should get these rooms cleaned out. I get a headache when I look inside."

"I wish I could find time to get the kid's clothes organized."

Teachers have a theory about the insides of their students' desks. It would be time consuming to prove, but in all likelihood it *would* be proven: The inside of a student's desk looks *just like his or her room*. If this revelation is bad news, it might be time to reorganize your home.

When a child falls completely apart over a cleanup job, it's often because the task seems insurmountable. Adults are no different. The thought of spending the weekend reorganizing every drawer and closet in your house is overwhelming. If this is a task that needs to be accomplished, break it into smaller units. Do one room a week, allowing two weeks for the kitchen. Give as many things to charity as possible. In a couple of months, your house will be streamlined—that in itself is a great guilt reducer!

Perhaps your house is already reasonably organized—with the exception of your children's rooms. Set aside a few hours, and try to involve your children in the process. Start by weeding out tired, broken and unused toys. Children enjoy preparing a bag for kids who are less fortunate, and the concept helps them appreciate what they have and others don't.

Use inexpensive shelving and plastic containers for toys and desk supplies. Make an effort to group and arrange things in a simple, logical manner. Store or give away clothing that is either too small or out of season. Organize the remaining clothes from your child's viewpoint, putting the most used items in easy-to-reach places. A clean, neatly arranged room is like a breath of fresh air to most children. If your child has been a part of the process, she just may go to school on Monday and attack her desk next!

School application

1. Organization of school desk and supplies sets the stage for good work habits.
2. A focus on neatness at home leads to neater school work.

Time-saving benefit

1. It takes less time to clean an organized house.
2. Because an organized home is easier to clean, the kids take on more of the work.

Guilt eraser

"Our clean, organized home helps my child desire and achieve order in his or her school environment."

Home responsibilities

What we say

"You have too many toys out at one time, and you're not using any of them."

"Muffy's out of fresh water again. I told you that dog was your responsibility!"

Guilty thoughts we think

"I should get them to clean up their things."

"I can't seem to get them to do their chores."

In Robert Fulghum's bestseller, ***All I Really Needed to Know I Learned in Kindergarten***, fourth and fifth on the list are "Put things back where you found them" and "Clean up your own mess." Though a tendency toward neatness may be innate, any child can learn these skills with your guidance.

The first step in guiding your child toward greater responsibility at home is to choose a task. There are two key questions to ask first: 1) Is the task appropriate for your child's age? 2) Is it a meaningful job, not just busy work?

Having chosen a task, *teach* your child how to do it properly. If you take time to supervise him initially, he will be more apt to do it correctly in your absence.

Then be *liberal* in your praise, *cautious* in your criticism. Try to state criticism in an encouraging manner, and base it more on effort expended than the end result. If 7-year-old Mandy has cleaned up 90 percent of her room, and all her mother notices (and talks about) is the remaining 10 percent, Mandy's motivation for subsequent clean-ups will evaporate.

Remarks such as the following may give children the boost they need to stay "on task." Some use an upcoming activity as a motivator.

> "You two got off to a great start cleaning up markers and crayons, so I'm going to help you finish."
>
> "When your room is clean, you may either get out a game or ride your bike."
>
> "Dinner will be ready in ten minutes, so please take your shower now."

Limiting certain activities to particular areas of the house can help avoid clean-up nightmares. Think about modeling clay. You really hate it, don't you? Your child started a love affair with it in pre-school, but it always seems to end up in your carpet. Restrict its use to an easily cleaned-up area of the house, and you may begin to love it, too. Other activities you may want to confine to designated areas are painting, markers, crafts and water play.

By teaching your child tasks he is capable of performing and helping him avoid clean-up disasters, you are setting him up for success in an area directly applicable to his school experience.

Next, help him follow through with his responsibilities by listing them, which will also help you avoid constant *verbal* reminders ("Mom's nagging again!"). Post a chart in a conspicuous place—the refrigerator often works well. (The chart on pp. 42 and 43 will give you ideas for jobs in such areas as laundry, personal hygiene, meal preparation and room cleaning.)

The sight of your child initiating and following up on these tasks will alleviate the guilt you feel over your busy schedule.

Who knows—with your children taking responsibility for more jobs at home, you may have time to do #11 on Robert Fulghum's list: "Live a balanced life—learn some and think some and draw and paint and sing and dance and play and work every day some."

School application

1. Students who maintain an orderly environment at school are more apt to stay on task.
2. Making a habit of completing *chores* on time helps make a habit of completing *school work* on time.

Time-saving benefit

1. Parents relinquish tasks such as making their children's beds.
2. The use of a chart makes constant verbal reminders unnecessary.

Guilt eraser

"By teaching my children to clean up after themselves and complete jobs at home, I've prepared them to be responsible in the classroom."

Consistent limits

What we say

"I've told you over and over to stop fighting with your brother!"

"You know better than to use that tone of voice with me!"

Guilty thoughts we think

"I should be able to get them to obey me."

"What will happen if they behave like this at school?"

When a teacher has a defiant or disrespectful student, he may arrange to meet with both the parent and child. When this conference takes place, an interesting thing happens. The child almost always addresses his parent in the same defiant or disrespectful manner that occasioned the conference in the first place. Sometimes that demeanor is such a habit that the parent fails to equate this behavior with the teacher's concerns. To prepare your child for school, and enjoy your life with him at home, *you must get him to obey you.* By skillfully teaching him obedience, you will, in turn, earn his respect.

In order to obey, your child must know, beyond a shadow of a doubt, what you expect of him. If you say, "I think you've watched enough television today," he will present a dissertation on why he feels otherwise. If, however, you look him in the eye and say, "I want you to turn the television off *now,*" your intent is clear. If you calmly repeat yourself in the face of arguments, pleading, and diversionary tactics, you will maintain authority.

As you give your child a clear message, your intuition will tell you whether she is going to be obedient. If you sense that she is going to disobey, or if she has already done so, calmly state the consequences of her actions. An ideal consequence is related to the situation and is unpleasant but not harmful:

> "Brian, you were supposed to call when you got to Brady's house. Since you didn't, you'll need to come home now, and you may not ride your bike to a friend's house for three days."
>
> "You two need to play that game without arguing. If you continue to fight, I will take the game away for a week."
>
> "Megan, if you continue to play with your food, you'll have to leave the table."

Many parents who are overworked, overtired and consumed by guilt address the discipline problem, but fail to follow through with the consequences. As one pediatrician put it, this failure causes an "incapacity to discipline in a consistent manner." It is of the utmost importance that you follow through with the consequences on a consistent basis. You *should not feel guilty* about giving your child a reasonable, carefully considered punishment. You are helping him learn to function within the limits he will encounter at school. At the same time, you are providing a more efficient and pleasant life at home.

A second-grade teacher with a boisterous class walks to the chalkboard and silently begins writing the names of students who are sitting quietly. An immediate hush falls over the room as the other students emulate the ones whose names are on the board. The teacher has quieted the entire class without saying one word!

Like these second-graders, your child wants to be recognized for being good. Verbal praise, a smile, a pat on the back, or a few special minutes together are all effective and meaningful ways to do so.

More tangible rewards may also be appropriate on an occasional basis. A child who is negligent about brushing her teeth might be motivated by a sticker chart taped up near the bathroom sink. After earning ten stickers for proper brushing, she might be given a suitable reward.

If you make a conscious effort to comment on good behavior, your positive reinforcement will become a habit.

School application

1. Kids who have consistent limits at home deal more successfully with limits at school.
2. Children who develop a respect for authority tend to have better rapport with adults at school.

Time-saving benefit

1. When children obey, daily events such as dressing and bathing take less time.

2. Discipline discussions and arguments are time-consuming and exhausting. Less of them means extra time for other things.

Guilt eraser

"By giving my child consistent discipline at home, I'm helping him behave at school."

Structure of eating

What we say

"Finish getting dressed or you won't have time for breakfast!"

"Well, okay, I guess we can drive through and get burgers again."

Guilty thoughts we think

"I should give her a healthier breakfast, but we're out of time."

"I shouldn't indulge them with food, but they've been good, and I'm so tired."

Dr. Victor Ince, a prominent Southern California pediatrician, believes that providing "optimal dietary conditions" is one of the three most important ways a parent can influence a child's health. These optimal conditions are a combination of a regular eating schedule and healthy foods.

When your child was one year old, his impatience with hunger knew no bounds. Though his tolerance has increased with age, he is still much more affected by hunger than an adult. Regularly scheduled meals help him to function well throughout the day. It is imperative that a child start out with a healthy breakfast. By 10 a.m., a teacher can readily spot the students who missed this meal. A bowl of sugar-free or low-sugar, whole grain cereal with milk and fruit is one quick and easy way to give your child a good start.

The structured nature of the school day assures that your child will have lunch on time. If buying lunch is financially feasible, it tends to make the morning a bit easier as everyone hurries to get ready.

If your child brings her lunch, teaching her how to pack it helps her learn responsibility and saves you time. Supervise her as she packs her lunch, and keep in mind that many schools discourage parents from sending sugary desserts.

> "Mom, can I have a snack?"
>
> "No, it's 4:30 and we'll be eating dinner soon."
>
> "But I'm starving. I can't wait. My stomach really hurts!"
>
> "Okay, you may have an apple."
>
> "But I don't want an apple. All I want is toast and jelly. Please Mom?"
>
> "Well, okay. But don't spoil your dinner."

Of course she *will* spoil her dinner, but it won't be *her* fault. Kids cannot last from lunch until dinner without eating. If you offer them a healthy snack immediately after school, they'll be hungry again by dinner time. Good, healthy snack ideas include yogurt, fruit, carrot sticks, cheese, and crackers with peanut butter. If you wait until they're starving, you may have to choose between spoiling their dinner and dealing with cranky, whiny kids.

Dinner time. We wish it could be like June and Ward Cleaver sitting down with Wally and "the Beav," but it usually isn't. However, by timing an afternoon snack, and serving dinner at a reasonable time, your children will be hungry, but not famished. This will give you the best shot at a pleasant ambience at the dinner table. Some other ideas:

1. Serve a variety of healthy foods in small portions. Draw from all four food groups, especially fruits and vegetables.
2. Foster good conversation by keeping the television off.
3. Praise good table manners.
4. Have dessert occasionally rather than routinely. It should not be the prime motivator for eating dinner.
5. Keep children at the table until *you* excuse them.

Sometimes the time pressures of work, school, day care, soccer practice and swimming lessons impinge on the dinner hour. On these nights, a well-balanced, home-cooked meal looms as an overwhelming task, and the nutritional disadvantage of fast food is an acceptable trade off for eating at a reasonable hour with a minimum of cleanup.

Caroline Dash, a Registered Dietician in the Southern California area, specializes in choosing the healthiest choices from a restaurant menu.

Cholesterol and sodium, she notes, are the main nutritional villains in most fast foods. The high fat content can fill kids with empty calories. Even if you're running late and don't have time to fix an elaborate dinner, her suggestions for quick and *healthy* meals—a selection of which are on page 36—are a much-preferred alternative to the "healthiest" fast food.

How can you dine on fast food without feeling pangs of guilt. Make smart choices! Pick smaller burgers with fewer condiments—always lower in fat than the jumbo version. Substitute juice or water for soft drinks. Or pick up the phone and order a cheese pizza—one of the lowest-fat fast food choices you can make.

School application

1. A good breakfast helps a child concentrate at school.
2. Healthy eating habits boost all-around health and increase school attendance.

Time-saving benefit

1. Serving dinner on time makes the evening less rushed.
2. Simple, healthy foods often require less preparation time.

Guilt eraser

"When I serve balanced, regular meals, my children stay healthier and develop sound, lifetime eating habits."

Structure of sleeping

What we say

"All right, but just 15 more minutes and then lights out!"

"You should have been up 15 minutes ago. Hurry or you'll miss the school bus!"

Guilt-Free Dinners In 15 Minutes

English Muffin Pizza

Tomato sauce, herbs, low fat mozzarella cheese, applesauce

Stir Fry Chicken & Vegetables

Cubed chicken breasts, sauteed with frozen chinese vegetables, (small amount of oil and soy sauce), instant rice

Soft Tacos

Seasoned ground turkey in heated flour tortilla, cheese, lettuce, tomatoes

Pasta with Cheese

Grated low fat cheese on pasta, green salad, sliced fruit

Pasta Salad

Leftover meat and pasta, low fat salad dressing, tomatoes, cucumber, etc., toasted cheese bread

Homemade Burritos

Vegetarian refried beans, "burrito bar" with low fat cheese, tomatoes, green onions, etc.

Deli Style Ham

Heated sliced ham, microwave baked potato, sliced raw vegetables

Tuna Burgers

Water packed canned albacore mixed with celery, light mayo on a wholewheat bun or in pita bread, slice of cheese, sprouts

Guilty thoughts we think

"I should get them to bed, but I haven't seen them much today."

"The kids are exhausted every morning, and we're always behind schedule."

Ask any elementary school teacher which subjects he schedules before lunch and which after. It's a sure bet that reading and math—the two subjects requiring the greatest concentration—are taught in the morning.

Teachers know that students tire during the course of the day, and that they do not learn as well when fatigued. To get through his busy school day with energy left for after school hours, your child must have adequate sleep.

Here is a general guide to the *average* hours of sleep required by age:

Age	Hours of Sleep Required
5-6	10-12
7-8	9-11
9-11	8-10

Do not consider this "gospel"—children of the same age may require more or less sleep than the above chart indicates. Go by your own knowledge of your child's behavior when he or she gets too much or too little sleep.

In addition to receiving an adequate amount of sleep, your child's sleep schedule should be as routine as possible. When kids stay up too late, their sleep schedule is disrupted. They either get up at the usual time and feel tired, or sleep late and then have trouble sleeping the next night.

Too basic?

Yes, because everyone knows it. No, because a myriad of problems make it difficult to get kids to bed on time. Here are suggestions to help avoid bedtime problems:

1. Think ahead and gear yourself up for the effort bedtime requires. If you procrastinate, you will be even more tired.
2. Be direct and consistent about bedtime so that your children will know that you mean business.
3. Vigorous physical activity during the day helps kids fall asleep more easily.
4. Avoid giving your child a job to do before going to bed. If the job is the lesser of two evils, your child will work slowly to avoid bed.
5. Once your child is in bed, eliminate two reasons to get up: Have your child use the bathroom first, and put an unspillable cup of water by his bed.
6. If your child has an object of security such as a blanket or an animal, tuck it in with him.
7. Spend a few minutes doing something special that you repeat each night. Such a ritual can hold a chaotic day together for a child. Sing a song, say a prayer, tell a story, or whisper three good things your child did that day.
8. Say "good night"...and mean it.

Putting kids to bed on time affects the entire next day. The morning is more pleasant because rested kids are more apt to get up on time. Children are able to learn more and perform better in school because they are more alert. They have energy left over for homework and fun at home. In an overall sense, their health is better because adequate rest strengthens their immunity to colds and viruses. Here's one last advantage: If they get to bed early, you might even get some time for yourself or your spouse!

School application

1. Regular sleep makes a child more alert for school and homework.
2. Sufficient sleep boosts the immune system, leading to better health—and better attendance.

Time-saving benefit

1. An early bedtime for the kids gives you (parents) more time for yourselves.
2. Rested children wake up more easily, decreasing morning time pressures.

Guilt eraser

"If I give my child regular and sufficient sleep, she will be mentally and physically alert at school."

Once structure and routine become a part of life at home, deviating from them becomes an occasional treat rather than a chaotic condition. Pediatrician Victor Ince describes this as "flexibility within consistency." Being consistent yet flexible means that Christopher's strict 7:30 bedtime can become 8:30 or even 9:00 when he spends the night at Grandma's house. Flexibility means that leftover pizza for breakfast is OK...once in a while.

McCall's describes a health-conscious mother who designates one week each year as "Yucky Cereal Week," during which her kids can eat whatever disgustingly unhealthy, sugar-laden cereal they like. Because her kids look forward to this one week, they don't complain about 51 weeks of *healthy* cereal. And because this mother is nutrition-conscious *most* of the time, she can enjoy one irresponsible week without feeling guilty.

Routine provides your children with security. Breaking it on occasion reinforces their cooperation and helps them to be flexible themselves.

Children *are* naturally pretty flexible—they readily adjust to changes in circumstances, moods, and rules. The most important thing to remember is that whether the change is major, such as a move or an addition to your family, or minor, such as a change in bedtime or homework schedule, kids will adapt if the situation is made clear:

> "We think that doing these things at home will help your work habits at school."
>
> "I'm hoping that more sleep each night will help you stay healthier."
>
> "I feel very tired after work, and I need you to take on more responsibilities at home."
>
> "Putting your own clothes away will help you learn how to keep your things neat at home and at school."

Kids don't want their parents to feel guilty, tired and frustrated. When Mom and Dad are happy, life is much more fun. Sarah will enjoy making her own lunch for the first time on Monday. By Thursday, it will be a tiresome chore. But if Sarah knows that it's helping her be more grown up, her mom to get ready for work in the morning, and that she can't get out of it anyway because Mom means what she says, at least it becomes a little easier to slap on the peanut butter and jelly.

"Hey, Jake. I can ride to the store with you because I got all my work done yesterday."

"I can't, Eric. I have to go right home from the bus stop."

"Well, I'll come by in an hour and then we can ride."

"Eric, I can't. I'm not allowed to play outside all week."

"Oh. What happened?"

"At Parent Conferences, Mrs. Green told my mother that I'm not handing in my work. She and my mom made this chart of all the things I have to do."

"Wow. That's too bad."

"Yeah. At first my mom was really mad but then we went and bought these cool stickers. Every time I complete my work, I get one. Plus my mom and dad helped me clean out my room. The worst part was they threw out my worm collection, but I found all my missing baseball cards!"

"Hey, that's great. Maybe I could come over next week to trade some cards."

"Sure. See you later, Eric."

Tasks That Will Help

Area	Jobs for Ages 5-7
Meal Preparation	1. Help put away groceries 2. Set the table 3. Perform simple kitchen tasks 4. Clear the dirty dishes
Laundry	1. Put dirty clothes in hamper 2. Separate colors for each person 3. Separate clean clothes 4. Put piles of clean clothes away
Personal Hygiene	1. Brush teeth with supervision 2. Wash self in bath 3. Wash hands before eating 4. Put on clean clothes
Bedroom	1. Make own bed 2. Keep toys and games neat 3. Keep desk supplies in order 4. Organize school bag and homework
Cleanup	1. Pick up toys in house 2. Pick up toys in yard 3. Help with general cleaning 4. Keep possessions in room

Your Children Learn

Job for Ages 8-11	School Application
1. Help make lunches 2. Prepare simple foods 3. Cook with supervision 4. Load the dishwasher	Kids stay healthier and are more likely to choose good foods at school.
1. Bring dirty clothes to washer 2. Operate washer and dryer 3. Put clean clothes away 4. Iron with supervision	Kids learn to take care of their things, keeping them clean and organized.
1. Brush own teeth 2. Take shower, wash hair 3. Maintain neat appearance 4. Dress appropriately.	Teachers and school personnel respond better to a child who is neat and clean.
1. Make bed, remove linens 2. Keep closet organized 3. Keep desk in order 4. Organize school bag and homework	A neat room leads to an organized school desk and homework.
1. Vacuum 2. Help with yard work 3. Dust 4. Help keep kitchen clean	Teachers and kids alike appreciate a student who cleans up after himself.

Chapter Three

Listening, Communicating & Self-Esteem

What does efficient communication have to do with involvement in the education of your children? The answer is simple: Absolutely everything!

How you communicate with your children and how they communicate with you sets a standard for how they talk and listen to their teachers and classmates.

When the avenues of communication between parent and child are clear and frequently used, the child feels good about himself. When a child feels good about himself, he behaves better at home and at school. Behaving at school enhances the learning process and makes the school run smoothly.

A child who whines, yells, argues, talks back, lacks self-esteem and fails to listen attentively, is disruptive to any classroom. The teacher has to take time away from teaching to attend to the needs of this particular child.

It also affects the attitude of the teacher toward the child. Although teachers are taught to treat all children the same, and they certainly try to do so, they are still imperfect human beings like the rest of us. A teacher can't help feeling a little negative about a child who is disrespectful, constantly interrupts, or seeks excessive attention. And the child's behavior will undoubtedly affect the teacher's attitude toward his or her parents, too.

In our changing world, parents are faced with more demands on their time than ever before. A detailed survey we mailed to hundreds of parents revealed that they wanted schools to teach self-esteem and communication skills. At the same time, *teachers* who responded to our survey said they believed *parents* needed to be more involved in promoting self-esteem and enhancing communication at home. Obviously, the solution to this seeming dilemma is for teachers and parents to become *partners* in this endeavor.

Effective listening

Dad has just returned from work. He's skimming the newspaper and watching the nightly news at the same time. His son, John, comes up to talk to him.

John: "I don't want to play soccer any more. I'm going to quit the team."

Dad: "No you're not. Anyway, you like soccer, and you're good at it."

John: "I am not. I hate it."

Dad: (looking at the TV) "Don't be silly."

John: "Dad, you're not listening. I don't want to play."

Dad: "Well, you're going to. You made the commitment, we paid the money, so you might as well make the best of it."

John: (under his breath) "Damn."

Dad: "Don't use that kind of language with me, young man. Go to your room!"

The next day at school, John speaks out of turn three times. He has to be told to stay in his seat, and he fails to complete his writing assignment.

John is neither a bad student nor a behavior problem, but lately he has seemed to need a lot more attention at school. The teacher tries to meet John's needs, but it isn't enough. She calls John's mom to tell her he's been having some difficulty lately. "John's a good kid," she concludes. "He just needs to concentrate a little more."

Later that day...

Mom: "John, I got a call from your teacher today. She said you're not paying attention in class, and you're not concentrating. What's wrong with you?"

John: "Nothing."

Mom: "What do you mean, nothing? If it was nothing, she wouldn't be calling me."

John: "Oh, she's dumb and always picking on me."

Mom: "She wouldn't be picking on you if you did what you were supposed to. I do not want any more calls from school. Do you hear me?"

John: "Yeah, okay."

John's mom and dad are very busy people. They each just had a brief conversation with their son, but there was little communication—neither parent was listening to what John had to say. And neither ever did find out what was *really* wrong. As a result, John goes to school seeking attention and attempting to get someone—*anyone*—to listen to him.

Listening is a skill that takes time to master. But once you acquire it, knowing how to listen will *save* time. Here are some steps to increase *your* listening skills:

1. ***Stop and take time to listen attentively.*** If you are busy, make arrangements to talk later. Do not try to listen to your child while you're doing something else.
2. ***Acknowledge what your child is saying.*** Most often, looking a child in the eyes and saying "Oh," "Un-huh" or "Really?" lets them know you heard what they said and encourages them to tell you more. Avoid jumping in with solutions to their problems. Kids don't like that—and, more often than not, the child will think your solution is "stupid" anyway.
3. ***Let your children know you understand*** what they are feeling by giving their feelings a name. Do not ask a child how she "feels"—she usually doesn't know. Saying "That must have made you angry," or "I can see how frustrated you are," or "You seem sad," tells a child that you heard what she said and you understand.
4. ***Don't minimize your child's feelings.*** They are real to the child, and your response must tell him it's *okay* to feel whatever he *is* feeling. At the same time,

> a child needs to know that he cannot always *act* on those feelings.

In a classroom, a child who listens accomplishes more. A teacher has more time available for teaching when she is not wasting it trying to get a child to listen, pay attention and follow through with directions. A parent's efforts to teach listening skills assist in the learning process in a positive and productive manner.

What was *really* wrong with John? Here's the way the conversation with his father might have gone if the above rules were followed:

John: "I don't want to play soccer any more. I'm going to quit the team."

Dad: (turning off the TV.and facing John) "Oh...you sound upset."

John: "I am! They added this new kid to the team."

Dad: "Oh."

John: "He thinks he's pretty good."

Dad: "Really?"

John: "I don't want him to take my position."

Dad: "Are you afraid he might?"

John: "Yeah...could you help me practice on Saturday?"

Dad: "Sure."

Teaching your child to listen to *you* is an equally essential skill. Schools must have enforceable rules in order to run smoothly. Parents who teach their children to listen contribute greatly to the educational process.

Problems can develop, however, when busy parents feel guilty regarding the limited time they have to spend with their children.

Mom: "Daniel, I told you two days ago to clean your room; it's still not done."

Daniel: "I will, Mom. But first let me help with making brownies."

Mom: (hesitating) "Oh, all right."

Mom: (later) "Now, go in and clean your room."

Daniel: (whining) "Just let me watch my favorite show first. Please!"

Mom: (hesitating again) "All right."

When the bell rings after recess the following day, all of the children are supposed to return the play equipment to the proper place and line up. Daniel continues to bounce the ball against the wall. Why should he stop? He has learned at home that although you are told what to do, you don't have to listen.

The teacher now has to attend to Daniel while neglecting her other students. When parents teach children to listen at home, the teacher's job is easier and the school runs smoother.

Mom: "Daniel, clean your room, please."

Daniel: "Oh, Mom. Let me help you first."

Mom: "I'll be making brownies in 15 minutes. If your room is clean, you may help. If not, you can't. Your first responsibility is your room."

Busy parents with limited time to spend with their children will find that when their kids listen to them, guilt is reduced and the quality of family time enhanced.

Nonverbal communication

One of the most powerful ways to communicate with children does not involve words. The message you send with your body, hand gestures and facial expressions often has more of an impact on your child than what comes out of your mouth.

Marie teaches freshman math at the local high school. By the time she grades papers, plans her lesson for the next day, and picks up her sons at their after-school sports program, it is 4:30. Her husband, Stan, comes home at 6:30. Marie finds that she talks nearly nonstop as she deals with her two sons, aged 7 and 9, during the two hours in between. Unfortunately, much of the talk is negative—nagging the boys about homework and chores and refereeing their arguments.

When Stan comes home, everything changes. In fact, Marie sometimes feels jealous of the way in which Stan gets the boys to listen to him. What does Stan do differently? Because of the way kids respond to Dad, some women have come to believe that men have magical powers. The fact is, they don't.

When the boys run through the kitchen playing cowboys and Indians, Marie yells, "I've told you over and over not to run in the house!" The boys *have* heard those words —so often they're immune to them. She is ignored.

When the boys run past Stan, however, he steps into their path and extends his hand to stop them. The stern expression on Stan's face tells the boys he means business. The running ceases. The nonverbal message Stan sent is not magic—merely clear, concise and effective communication.

Nonverbal cues are just as effective in conveying a positive message. Eight-year-old Ricky has just finished a grueling homework assignment in spelling. If his Mom says, "Good job, Ricky. I like the way you finished your spelling," she has reinforced his action. If she holds up her hand for a "high five," and follows it with a smile and a hug, Ricky gets the same message.

Sometimes parents say one thing but convey an entirely different message with their body language. This mixed message is confusing and irritating to children. Nine-year-old Karen rushes home from a neighborhood baseball game. She bursts into the kitchen where her mother is cooking dinner and feeding the baby.

"Guess what, Mom? I just hit a home run right over Joey's head!" "Good for you," answers her mother in a distracted voice, as she tries to get the baby to take one more spoonful of pears. Her choice of words is fine, but her monotone delivery and lack of eye contact tell Karen that hitting the home run was not such a big deal after all. Disappointed, Karen walks away and turns on the TV.

Nonverbal communication is a powerful mode of expression. It is especially valuable for busy parents who find themselves exhausted at the end of the day. With a look, parents can stop children dead in their tracks; with a smile and a hug, they can chase away the blues. When parents feel guilty and discouraged, much of their evening's conversation consists of nagging the kids. Nonverbal communication can strengthen, even replace your words.

Promotion of self-esteem

What is self-esteem? It is how a person feels about himself. That judgement affects the kinds of friends he chooses, the choices he makes, and how productive he will be. It also affects his creativity, integrity, stability and whether he will be a leader or a follower.

A child's feeling of self-worth determines the use she makes of her aptitudes and abilities. A child's success in life is influenced more by self-esteem than whether that child is an "A" or "C" student. A teacher who has students who feel good about themselves, finds them a joy to teach.

Promoting self-esteem is the single most important gift a parent can give a child. If a child who brings home a "C" on a writing assignment is told, "I know you worked really hard on that paper. The second paragraph was very clever and I liked it a lot," he or she will return to school motivated, challenged and ready to work.

Parents can actively promote self-esteem on five levels:

The first level is ***attitude.*** Gene Bedley writes in the ***ABCD's of Discipline,*** "If you treat an individual as he is, he will stay as he is; if you treat him as if he were what he ought to be and could be, he will become what he ought to be and could be."

If you communicate to your child that he or she is lazy, your child *will* be lazy at home and at school. On the other hand, if you communicate that he or she is special, unique and able, the work he or she produces in school will reflect *that* opinion.

The belief you have about your child determines how the child views himself.

A parent's positive attitude makes a child feel confident. A confident child works responsibly, independently and cooperatively. A parent who has instilled a positive attitude has contributed to the child's success at school.

The second level is ***praise.*** Everyone feels good when they receive praise for a job well done. The important thing to remember about praise is that it should deal with the child's efforts and accomplishments. For some, the tendency is to focus more on what we and others do *in*correctly, so that little attention is given to what is done *correctly*. Children thrive on encouragement, and your praise will show in your child's enthusiasm at school.

The third level is ***feelings.*** When we accept a child's feelings, we accept him. A child who feels accepted, understood and loved has high self-esteem. When a child expresses his feelings, he is telling you who he is. When we openly accept those feelings, we validate him and make him feel secure. In school, an insecure child needs constant attention from school personnel and places too much unnecessary strain on those individuals.

The fourth level of self-esteem involves remembering that ***people and actions are separate.*** In ***Children: The Challenge,*** Dr. Rudolf Dreikurs says, "We must make a particular effort to separate the deed from the doer." Parents must separate their child's behavior from her thoughts and feelings; otherwise, the child's self-worth sinks with each mistake.

Children *learn* from their errors. "Rick, I don't like the way you pushed in line. You're too nice a boy to do that." In this example, Rick can easily change his behavior while still maintaining a good feeling about himself. If, on the other hand, Rick was told he was a pushy kid, seeing himself as "pushy" could cause problems at school.

A child who is told she is bossy, lazy, stupid, irresponsible or dumb, will not try hard in a learning situation because she believes her goals are unattainable.

Communication is the fifth level of self-esteem. Parents who can communicate their feelings have kids who can express their feelings and wants in a positive way.

Teacher: "Mary, you're not getting your work done. Is something wrong?"

Mary: (silence)

Teacher: "I can't help you if you can't tell me what's wrong."

Mary: "Nothing..."

Teacher: "Jennifer, you're not getting your work done. Is something wrong?"
Jennifer: "Tracy hurt my feelings at recess."
Teacher: "Oh, and that upset you?"
Jennifer: "Yeah. She's supposed to be my best friend."
Teacher: "I see. You're feeling hurt?"
Jennifer: "Yes, but I'll be okay."

Jennifer's ability to communicate her feelings, and the teacher's ability to listen, allowed the problem to be identified and solved quickly and efficiently.

Conversational skills

Nationally known child psychologist James Dobson describes conversational skills as analogous to playing catch. When you ask a question or make a comment, you are throwing the ball to the other person. As they either answer your question or acknowledge your comment, they are catching the ball. To continue the game, the other person must then throw the ball back to you by asking another question or commenting further. If one participant wants to do all of the catching and not bother with the throwing, the other will eventually lose interest.

Some old friends join you for dinner. You are anxious for them to meet your 8-year-old son, Justin. As you introduce Justin to your friends, they make an effort to draw him out, asking him several questions about school and sports. To your dismay, Justin gives one-word answers while looking down at his tennis shoes.

Is Justin a sullen child? Does he have bad manners? Is he too insecure to talk to a new adult? The answer to all of these questions is probably "No." He just hasn't developed his conversational skills. Initiating and participating in conversation is a skill that anyone can learn. Here are some basic points:

1. Look the other person in the eye to show that you are interested.
2. "Play ball," being conscious of the give and take of conversation.
3. Ask pertinent questions. Most people open up quickly when given a chance to talk about themselves.
4. Try to make these questions open-ended as opposed to "yes/no" (closed) questions.
5. Use short phrases such as "really" and "uh-huh" to show that you are listening.

With some imagination, you can make it fun for your child to learn these conversational skills. Choose someone at the dinner table to describe the best thing that happened to them that week. Let everyone else at the table ask the person an open-ended question about it. Kids thrive on this type of structured talk.

Perhaps you could practice phone conversations with your child, or let two children role play a situation. Teaching your child to be a good conversationalist will enhance his or her relationships with teachers and peers.

When parents send a child to school with positive self-esteem, listening skills, and the ability to converse, they form a partnership with the school. What better way for them to be actively involved in their children's education?

Some parents are simply too busy to volunteer in the classroom. You may be one of them. *It doesn't matter if you can't spare the time*—any guilt can be erased if you have successfully taught your child the skills discussed in this chapter.

Part Two

Time For School

Chapter Four

The Busy Parent and School Involvement

In the preceding chapters, we discussed parental involvement at home and how that involvement serves to enhance the education of our children. Participation on that level helps busy parents aid the school by sending off children who are better equipped to successfully handle their school environment.

Why, then, do so many parents who successfully organize their homes, who provide environments that enhance self-esteem and listening, and who read religiously to their children, still feel guilty?

Because they are told they are still not contributing enough.

As parents of the '90s, we are told over and over to do more and more. Enrichment at home is not enough. We are supposed to help at school and assist the teachers so our children can gain the maximum benefit from their school experience.

The PTA

The Parent Teachers Association claims that *no* parent is too overwhelmed or too alienated to become involved in some way.

Tell that to Mary, a single mother with three kids. She gets up at 6:00 a.m., makes breakfast and prepares two lunches. She makes sure her 11-year-old has his homework, reminds her 6-year-old to take beans and popcorn to school for a special project, and helps her 4-year-old get his shoes on. And they're off. She drops the older two at the bus stop and rushes to the pre-school to drop off her youngest. By 8:30 a.m. she's at work.

At 4:45 p.m., Mary finds herself rushing once again. She must get to the pre-school to pick up the 4-year-old, go to the after-school day care to pick up the 6-year-old, and then hurry to the soccer field to catch a few minutes of her older son's soccer practice.

By 5:45, she is heading home, but her evening is just beginning. She has dinner to fix, homework to supervise, laundry, baths, and, hopefully, some time left over to read, listen and communicate with her kids. At 9:00, all is quiet.

As Mary sits down to relax and have a cup of tea, she goes through notices her children have brought home from school. She begins reading the PTA newsletter. And what's Mary's first reaction as she peruses it? ***Guilt!***

That's right. The PTA is looking for volunteers to help with the school carnival and requesting that parents attend a local school board meeting as a show of support for a new initiative. A couple of classes need room mothers, and they need lots of goodies to sell at the upcoming bake sale to raise money for some much-needed library books.

Mary also feels guilty as she reads the names of friends and neighbors who have contributed and helped out at PTA functions during the past month.

"I wish I had more time," she sighs to herself. She's feeling guilty for not participating more...but how...and when?

Mary decides to volunteer for an hour at the school carnival, selling popcorn. Although she has to squeeze this in between other commitments and responsibilities, she feels good about volunteering. At the school carnival, Mary overhears two other mothers talking:

> "How long have you been here?"
>
> "I was here yesterday setting up all afternoon and got here this morning at 8:00 a.m."
>
> "Yeah, I was up late baking cookies and then I picked up extra tables this morning. I'll probably be here all day."
>
> "Me, too."

Mary's guilt resurfaces—she obviously has not done enough!

Mary is not atypical. She, like thousands of other parents, feels those familiar pangs of guilt as she attempts to shoehorn PTA activities into an already overcrowded schedule of work, chores, errands and taxi service.

The scope of the PTA is immense. Members are involved in everything from providing special programs for preschoolers to holding workshops on parent education to setting up after-school day care. They organize special science, art and literature programs for kids. They coordinate special events and fundraisers and work politically for changes needed to provide the best environment for learning. All of this involves volunteer support. Parents receive a neverending stream of "help" letters.

For busy parents, however, the demands of the PTA can be overwhelming. There seem to be so *many* activities and projects and so *many* requests for volunteers that many parents shy away from any involvement at all. Guilt rears its ugly head when parents waste precious time feeling badly because their schedules simply won't allou them to do more.

Interestingly, our interviews with and surveys from teachers revealed encouraging news for busy parents.

First, we need to stress that we wholeheartedly support the time and effort the PTA puts forth to help children in thousands of schools nationwide. However, the purpose of this book is to help already-busy parents use whatever time they have left in the best way possible. Our research indicates that out of six areas in which parents can be involved—reading to your child, promoting self esteem, homework, volunteering at school, assisting with projects and being involved with the PTA—teachers rated PTA involvement last.

This is not to say that the PTA is not important, merely that educators felt that out of these six areas, busy parents needed to focus their attention on those that were more child centered.

A parent who has one child in school and two at home may find that there are only one or two extra hours available per week to devote to school-related activities. If that parent uses all of that time to volunteer in the library and to help organize a PTA-sponsored art program, there won't be any time left for reading, listening or promoting self esteem.

And *excessive* PTA involvement can be a problem. A parent who is frequently at school may begin taking charge of responsibilities that should rightly fall on her child's shoulders. Your child is a link between home and school. School is the first place a child begins to have some responsibility for himself. A parent who is frequently at school working with the PTA, may find herself picking up her child's homework assignments, bringing home a sweatshirt that was left behind, or picking up notices that the child should be bringing home.

Doing all this will neither help your child gain autonomy nor experience the pride of independence. Your child needs these skills to be successful at school. We are not saying "don't be involved." Go ahead and be *very* involved if you have the time. Just do not incorporate your child's responsibilities into your own.

There are several ways the PTA can aid the busy parent. The PTA can tell you "who's who" at the school—important for busy parents because knowing who does what will save you time. If there is a problem or concern, you will know exactly whom to go to. Parents can waste valuable time going to a teacher to discuss something the teacher can do nothing about. This information is readily available at the beginning of the school year.

The PTA also provides parents with a timetable of the school day and upcoming events. This enables a busy parent to plan ahead—incorporating school programs and activities into your schedule reduces stress and guilt.

One father who was unable to attend an awards ceremony in which his daughter was receiving a special certificate had the program taped. Later, as the family watched the video together, the father said, "Although I couldn't come to the program, I'm glad I got to see you get this special award. It means a lot to me, and I am very proud of you." The little planning it took to arrange for the video was a very effective way for this father to be involved.

School involvement opportunities

As was mentioned earlier, many busy parents fail to get involved at all because they fear they will be asked to do more than their schedules allow. It is very important to know how much time you have and to be very specific about what you can do.

Parents who attempt to squeeze in too much will feel the tug of guilt if they find that their involvement in school activities is leaving them with no quality time for their children. Of course, we can feel just as guilty by doing nothing at all.

The following are ways in which even busy parents can involve themselves in their children's school activities:

Bake sales—A busy parent can stop at a bakery and pick up a dozen cookies.

Trip chaperone—Pick one field trip per semester. Hint: Morning-only trips require less time commitment.

Phone calling—This can be accomplished during evening hours.

Attend school functions—It's especially important to make arrangements to attend programs in which your child plays an important role.

Provide needed supplies for classroom and PTA projects—The school and PTA will be glad to give you a list of needed supplies that you can shop for and deliver to the school.

Provide prizes and awards—This usually means just a few phone calls to local businesses for donations and, perhaps, a quick shopping trip.

Ticket sales—A commitment that might take only one hour a semester.

Publicity for special events—Phone calls over a couple of nights or creating and handing out flyers.

Food donations for luncheons—If you enjoy cooking, you can turn this into a fun project and involve your kids. Or you can easily just buy prepared platters of cold cuts, salads, etc. to drop off at the school.

Guest speaker—Talk on career day, a commitment that may involve less than an hour of your time.

Teach a special subject—This may take more time but can be rewarding if the topic is of great interest to you.

Tutor—Time allocated can be entirely based on your availability.

Assist in the library—You can volunteer your time in the library or assist with record keeping.

Cut out materials—Another assignment that is easily squeezed in. You can be cutting out materials while your child reads or does homework.

Computer services—For those of you who have computers and enjoy working with them, you can design flyers and bulletins for upcoming events.

Make cassettes for reading—When you read to your child, you can record it and send it to school. It takes no extra time.

Don't look at this list and think you need to do it all. Remember, we are *eliminating* useless guilt. Participate whenever and however you can. Doing nothing promotes guilt. Doing *some*thing sends a message to your child that school activities and functions are important. The inherent message in any involvement is that you value the educational system and support its efforts.

Several teachers we interviewed said that one of the most important ways parents can be involved is to attend all activities in which their children are participants, which sends two messages—that we appreciate the school and the PTA for providing the program and that we support our children's participation.

Classroom/teacher involvement opportunities

> "The alliance between parents and teachers is a powerful influence and can reinforce common goals for children."
>
> —***Parents and Teachers*** by Doreen Croft

Parents send their children off to school with great expectations. One of those expectations is that teachers will take their children on an enlightened journey of learning. Busy parents also look to teachers to maintain the emotional well-being of their children. In order for teachers to successfully accomplish those goals, they need help.

Even with the advent of high technology, teachers have hectic and demanding schedules. They have to instruct, prepare lesson plans, handle discipline and student behavior, communicate effectively with students, parents, and school personnel, complete administrative responsibilities, and tackle endless amounts of paperwork. Teachers frequently proclaim their need for parents to help out. A recent survey by the National Education Association (NEA) found that more than 90 percent of teachers want parent involvement.

Parents, on the other hand, respond to that need with guilt! Whether they are full-time homemakers or attempting to balance a career with the responsibilities of home and family, they are struggling to manage their own responsibilities with a limited amount of time.

Both parents and teachers agree that for the sake of our children, a partnership is essential to maximize the learning experience. The following is a list of ways to accomplish that goal:

- An overwhelming number of teachers reported that the single most important thing a parent can do is to ***show an interest*** on a daily basis. Ask to see your child's work and go over it with him.
- ***Reinforce academics at home***. Maintain a positive attitude regarding the school system and the teachers. A busy parent can be involved in this manner without sacrificing time.
- ***Let the teachers know your schedule and availability.***
- ***Attend conferences.*** If you cannot attend in person, call the teacher and discuss the conference with your child. This emphasizes to the child your commitment to his education.
- ***Communicate any special needs.*** A teacher who is made aware of special circumstances —e.g., a recent move or divorce—can deal with a child in a more effective way.
- ***Avoid blaming the teacher.*** When problems arise, a teacher who is an advocate will work *with* you to reach a solution.

- ***Acknowledge the teacher's efforts.*** When a teacher has done something helpful to you or your child, make a point of thanking her. Most PTAs have teacher appreciation luncheons. Try to attend (or send a note).
- ***Set a good example for your child*** by exhibiting an attitude of respect toward the teacher. A parent who is courteous and polite most likely sends a child to school who demonstrates those same traits.
- ***Visit the class.*** This is not always possible for a busy parent. However, most teachers are appreciative of any parental visit. Attempt to come to class at least once a semester to observe. You'll see, firsthand, what goes on in the classroom and how your child performs and interacts.
- ***Provide needed materials.*** Throughout the school year, notices are sent home with requests for necessary "extras." Your donations take little time and are greatly appreciated. Sending goodies for class parties is an easy way to contribute.
- ***Assist with class projects.*** This could involve making reading cassettes, creating flash cards, cutting out materials, making lettering charts or similar activities.

Most parents don't realize that many teachers spend a lot of free time and some of their own money to provide special events and projects for their children. So *any* parental donation of time and effort will be appreciated.

One mother who worked full-time called her son's teacher at the beginning of the school year. She explained that she had no extra time during school hours to volunteer, but she did want to help. The teacher asked if she could help make some lettering charts. She didn't need them for two months, so the mother could complete the project at her leisure. During this ten-minute conversation, they also arranged a parent-teacher meeting convenient for both of them. Although this mother has a very restricted time schedule, she has eliminated useless guilt by contributing what she can.

One teacher we interviewed had this to say: "It may seem like you aren't doing much, but anything you do, big or small, gives a teacher more time to teach your child."

Overinvolvement and burn-out

You probably know someone like Cathy. She always seems to be at school—in the classroom, in the library, volunteering after school, assisting with every activity. She's on all the committees. She even writes the PTA newsletter. Cathy never seems to be walking—she's always running, apparently hurrying from one function to another.

You also know Cathy's kids. Most likely they are at your house after school and on weekends. They often have trouble listening and following rules.

The teachers know Cathy's kids, too. Although they are not bad kids, they appear to need an excessive amount of attention. It's not uncommon for them to come to school without their homework or with incomplete assignments.

To the outside world, Cathy is the epitome of a good parent involved in the educational process. In reality...she is not! When we see Cathy at school, we see an energetic, active woman seemingly very involved in her children's education. What we don't see is her suffering from late-night headaches or the back and neck pain she feels several times a week. We also don't see her impatience with her children as she struggles to stay involved in everything while neglecting vital areas of family life.

Cathy suffers from over-involvement and burn-out. She may be a bit of a caricature, but guilt often drives parents like Cathy to do many things without thinking whether these activities are effective.

Cathy is a concerned parent who recognizes the importance of playing an active role in her children's education. She is not, however, using her time in the most efficient manner to benefit her children and assist them in being as successful as possible. She may be helping the school and the PTA enormously, but she is at risk of burning out quickly.

Conscientious parents who understand the importance of parental involvement may jump into committing themselves without stopping to think about how *best* to utilize their time. Parents say that they used to be active at school, but now they don't seem to have the time. It's important to remember that kids don't just need your involvement for the first two years of school. They need it *throughout* their school years. When you volunteer too much and begin to resent it, you will burn yourself out and your children will fail to get the benefit of your ongoing support.

Busy parents need to sit back and assess their situation. Is the time you are devoting to school-related activities benefiting your child? Cathy's headaches are causing her to be impatient with her children. Her excessive time away from home does not allow her to monitor her children's homework. Overinvolvement is thwarting her efforts to enhance her children's education.

The symptoms of over-involvement may be similar to others brought on by stress:

Physical reactions

Dry throat/jaw tension
Neck and shoulder pain
Cold hands and feet, sweaty
palms, increased perspiration
Headaches
Frequent colds or flu
Uneasy stomach
Muscle cramps
Insomnia

Emotional reactions

Depression
Overeating
Loss of appetite
Decreased sex drive
Difficulty making decisions and
concentrating
Anxiety
Increased anger and irritability
Excessive crying

When you begin to suffer—either physically or emotionally—because of excessive involvement, you need to reevaluate your priorities. Overinvolvement and burn-out occur when a parent tries to do too much with too little time. For children to gain the most from your involvement, the balance between school commitments and parental responsibilities must be maximized.

When to say "yes" and when to say "no"

One of the most difficult words to say in the English language is "no." Even when you *want* to say it.

As Barbara finishes up the dinner dishes, Jessica, 6, and John, 3, are marauding through the house. Frank, Barbara's husband, is upstairs running a bath for the kids. Barbara is rushing because she wants to finish and help Jessica with her numbers and read to both kids before they go to bed. The telephone rings. It's Ann, the room mother in Jessica's class.

Ann: "Hi. I'm calling about the class party on Thursday and I need volunteers. Can you come to class at 10 and help set up? I also need some cookies and some construction paper for a special project."
Barbara: "Thursday? Well, okay, I'll be there."
Ann: "Great. Thanks. See you Thursday."

Barbara hangs up the phone and begins to feel angry and resentful. She attends school part-time and has a big exam on Friday. She was going to study on Thursday. She also doesn't have child care for John and can't take him to school with her because he disrupts the class.

Barbara feels she's just been in a no-win situation. If she had said "no," she'd feel guilty for not contributing. But saying "yes" makes her feel guilty, too. She needs to find time to study. She also has to find a sitter for John.

Barbara now finds herself yelling at her kids to hurry up and get ready for bed. She reads a quick story and is impatient with them when they try to tell her about their day. She wants the kids out of her hair so she can study.

There is a notion today that we should all be "super parents," able to "do it all," even if that sometimes means being in four places at once. Forget it.

It's impossible to be everything, to be everywhere, and to say yes to everyone. We are not made of rubber. When we stretch ourselves too far, we break.

Barbara's intentions are noble. She wants to contribute to the classroom and be involved with Jessica. However, failing to assist Jessica with her numbers and not listening to her does little to help Jessica be as successful as she can be in school. Volunteering in the classroom is great, but in Barbara's case, it is not the most effective way for her to be involved.

Barbara is justified in saying "no." Because she can't volunteer her time, she could offer to send supplies with Jessica to school. She could bake or buy goodies needed for the party. She could also contact the room mother and tell her when she *can* be available based on her schedule. Telling the person in charge that you need some advance notice can be helpful in organizing time and making necessary arrangements.

Parents too often view school involvement as a "yes" or "no" proposition—all or nothing.

Well, nothing could be further from the truth. There *are* only 24 hours in a day. If your involvement in school takes all your extra time, other areas vital to your child's growth will be neglected.

It is also important for your children to see you using your time efficiently. When they see you making choices or organizing your priorities, they will follow your example.

Some children also resent the time their parents spend away from home. They wonder why Mom is always at school working on a project and not home helping them.

If you say "yes" to school so often that you know the school secretary better than you know your own kids, it's time to reevaluate. Sometimes saying "no" to some things actually enables you to be a more effective partner in the home/school relationship.

Here are some guidelines to assist you in knowing when to say "yes" and when to say "no:"

- ***Remind yourself of your priorities.*** Will attending meetings three evenings a week for the fund-raising committee help your child more than working with her on her science project?
- ***Recognize and accept your limitations.*** If you're a working parent, you *know* you can't volunteer mornings in the library, no matter how often "volunteers needed" signs are posted there!
- ***Know your strengths and weaknesses.*** If you are a terrible cook, don't volunteer to bake. If creativity is not your thing, don't agree to help design an art project. If you've got business contacts, however, you may find soliciting sponsors for the school auction a project custom-made for your volunteer energies.
- ***Find out what the school's priorities are.*** And attempt to coordinate them with yours.
- ***Check your schedule.*** If you planned ahead from the beginning of the year, coordinating your schedule with the school's needs, you've probably already filled in volunteer activities. It's easier to say "no" to another commitment when you're already committed to an equally valuable activity.

Parents who feel guilty whenever they say "no" need to remember that "no" is not always a *negative* word. Just as "yes" is not always a *positive* word.

Saying "no" in some circumstances enables us to balance work, quality time with our children, school involvement, personal relationships, and time for ourselves.

If too much time is allotted to one area to the exclusion of another—regroup!

Chapter Five

The Busy Parent and School Communication

Communication between the home and the school is a two-way process. A continuous exchange of information helps to solidify the parent/teacher partnership.

Unfortunately, teachers grapple with large classes, and parents juggle the demands of work and home. When time constraints cause this two-way communication to become rare or infrequent, parents feel guilty because they are out of touch.

The key to strong home/school communication for the busy parent is using limited time productively to get answers and solve problems. Familiarity with the structure of a school district and basic modes of communication, such as conferences and report cards, helps parents work *with* the school in an efficient, time-saving manner.

Structure of a school district

Linda Cunningham glanced nervously at her watch. She needed to be home by 2:30, when the bus would drop off her first-grader. Lately, her part-time job as a loan officer was inching closer to full-time. Cradling the phone to her shoulder, she waited for the regional manager of the bank to take her call.

"Can you believe this?" Linda whispered to Cindy, the loan officer at the next desk. "I've worked for this bank for five years, all I want is an extended maternity leave, the baby is due in six weeks, and I don't have approval yet."

"Couldn't you take care of it through the department manager?" asked Cindy.

Linda rolled her eyes. "I thought that our immediate supervisor would be able to grant it, but when I filled out all of the paperwork for the department manager, he said that I needed to talk to the branch manager. Well, after two phone calls and one meeting with *her,* I found out that the regional manager is the only one who can approve extended leaves. Everyone has been nice, but I've wasted too much time going through three levels of management. And I can't stay on hold any longer or I won't be there when Timmy gets home from school." Linda hung up the phone and hurriedly left the office.

"Guess what, Mom?" yelled Timmy, slamming the door on his way into the kitchen. "They're moving the bus stop all the way over to Oak Street. Now I'll be able to walk really far with the guys every day!" Timmy handed his mother the announcement from the school.

Linda groaned as she read the letter. "That's just too far, Timmy. I'm going to get that bus stop moved back."

As Linda attempts to change this school-related decision, she finds herself going through an organizational structure quite similar to the one she encountered in her business environment. Once again, she will waste precious time taking an indirect route to the person who has the authority and expertise to answer her question.

On Monday, Linda took Timmy to school, hoping to get a few minutes with his teacher. Mrs. Jackson was understanding, but unable to help. "I wouldn't want my son to walk that far, either," she said. "Why don't you talk to the vice-principal about it?"

Now late for work, Linda waited anxiously for the vice-principal to end a phone conversation. "Your concerns are valid, Mrs. Cunningham," he explained. "I think the principal has had several complaints about that bus stop. He's not in today, but perhaps you could make an appointment with him for some time next week."

Reluctant to take any more time off work, Linda called the principal from her office. After a 15-minute conversation, Linda knew more about the bus stop problems, but was no closer to a solution. She took the principal's advice and called the school district office.

At last, she finally got the right person on the phone—the individual who handled transportation for the whole district. He explained that the bus stop had been moved because of some residents' complaints, but that he had heard from several parents who shared Linda's concern. He promised to talk with those residents and get back to Linda with some alternatives.

Once again, Linda was satisfied by the end result, but frustrated by the process.

School districts differ in size and specifics. Most, however, share an organizational pyramid much like that of many businesses. As in business, vertical "line" positions denote levels of authority. This structure is given a horizontal dimension by the "staff" or specialized positions

The charts on pp. 78 and 79 show typical organizational pyramids for business and a school district.

Information about your school district is available to you at the beginning of the school year. Becoming familiar

Structure For Business or Industry

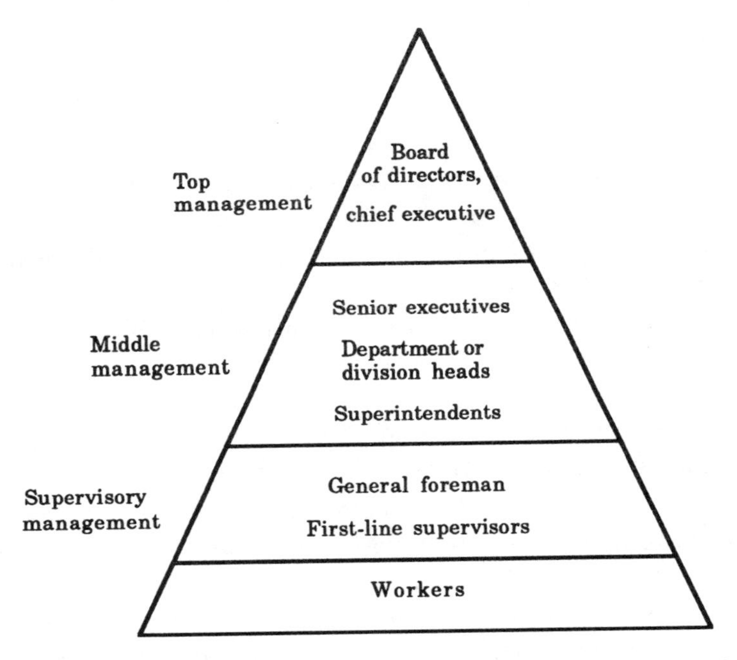

Source: Knezevich, Stephen J., Administration of Public Education, Harper & Row, NY, 1975, p. 42. Source also cites Dalton E. McFarland.

---

with your particular district will help you meet the educational needs of your child in a timely manner.

Proper channels for dissatisfaction

In elementary school, your child will have at least seven teachers, probably more. In junior high, she might have as many as 20. Odds are, you will not respect, admire and agree with every one of them. Between 5 percent and 10 percent of all teachers are incompetent, according to Bill Honig, California's State Superintendent of Public

Structure for a School District

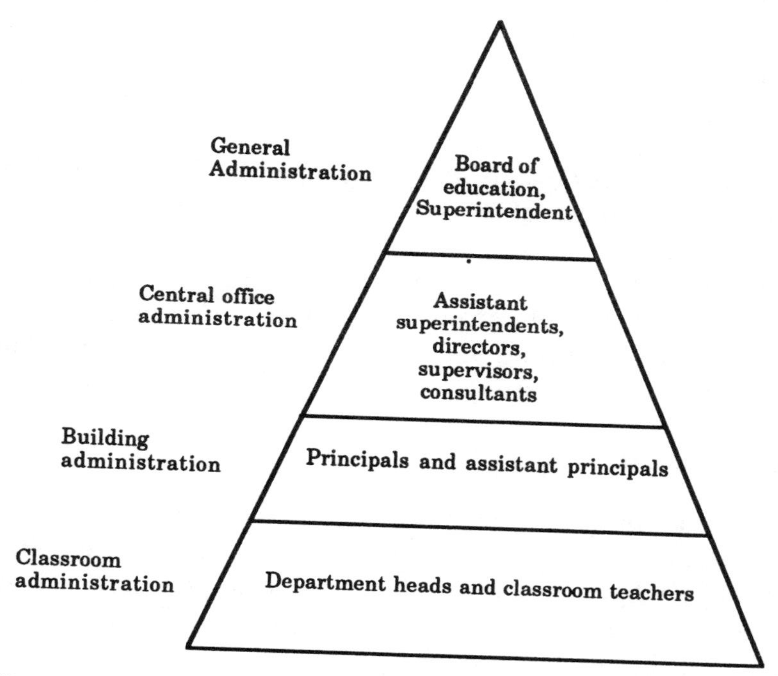

Source: Knezevich, Stephen J., Administration of Public Education, Harper & Row, NY, 1975, p. 42. Source also cites Dalton E. McFarland.

Instruction. Your child may have a very poor teacher or an excellent teacher with whom you simply disagree. When the inevitable problem does materialize, it is important to follow the right course of action.

Here are some guidelines to prevent wasted time:

Put everything in perspective

Your fourth-grader comes home from school devastated. Tearfully, she explains that when the class chose sides for the spelling bee, she was picked last.

Sympathizing with your daughter's spelling difficulties, you are furious with the teacher for choosing teams in such a hurtful manner. Angrily, you pull out the phone book to make an appointment with the principal.

Stop! Wait! Your hasty actions might cause more harm than good. At the very least, you will feel silly if your daughter has forgotten about the spelling bee by dinner time, and you're scheduled to meet with the principal before work the next morning.

Your child must learn to deal with the small problems and inequities of life at school. Letting a day or two pass before acting can help you decide whether or not an issue is really worth pursuing.

Start with the teacher!

Think about your own job. Imagine that a person with a complaint related to your area of responsibility has completely bypassed you, going instead to your supervisor. When your supervisor calls you in, it is likely that you will feel both threatened and angry.

When your child's teacher finds a note from the principal in her box that reads, "Please see me regarding method of choosing teams for spelling bee," she experiences several negative emotions. The most prevalent one is probably anger at *you* for going straight to the principal.

So don't take the second step before you try the first—talk to the teacher. If you start with the teacher, but do not get a satisfactory answer or solution, *then* it may be necessary to go over the teacher's head. In ***The National PTA Talks to Parents,*** Melitta Cutright cautions, "...going to a higher level will probably mean that you will never be able to develop a close relationship with that teacher."

Obviously, you would like to avoid killing any chance you have for establishing a good relationship with your child's teacher. If the issue is critical, however, it *may* be necessary, even advisable, to sacrifice that relationship to the needs of your child.

Be sensitive

Presuming you do have to discuss a problem with a teacher, you can influence the degree of defensiveness in him or her by the way you present your complaint. It is not to your advantage, for example, to use an accusatory tone. One new teacher in her early 20s received a scathing letter from a parent of one of her elementary students. The parent accused the teacher of giving too much homework, allowing her child little time for family activities and play.

The teacher realized that she was a bit overzealous and that *the parent was probably right.* But the tone of the letter lingered with her throughout the year, affecting her relationship with both child and parent.

How much better it would have been if the parent had calmly approached the teacher and said something like, "I'm having a problem with the amount of homework you're assigning." They could have arrived at a mutually acceptable solution without leaving a bitter aftertaste.

Realize that your child may be wrong

Sometimes kids mix up the facts, perceive a situation incorrectly, or simply lie. It is extremely frustrating for a teacher to have clear evidence of a child's cheating, for example, only to face a parent who will not even consider the possibility that his child might have done such a thing.

And while cases of out-and-out lying might be the exception, it is certainly not unusual for a 5- or 7- or 10-year-old to have completely misunderstood what a teacher has said or done.

Keep this in the back of your mind as you attempt to solve your conflict. It is embarrassing and disheartening to aggressively go to bat for your child, only to find out that she did not describe the situation accurately. Better to acknowledge and deal with whatever your child is feeling —something that *is* real and valid, whatever his or her misunderstandings—but give the teacher the benefit of the doubt when you approach him or her to discuss it.

Know the structure of your school district

Basic school district organization was discussed in the previous section. Your child's school office or the central district office will provide information about the structure of your particular district. You should be able to find out specific job titles and responsibilities as well as the names and phone numbers of the individuals holding those positions. Try to have this information on hand before it becomes necessary to use it. This will allow you to move through the proper channels in a deliberate but expedient manner.

Know your rights

In ***Help Your Child Make the Most of School,*** award-winning teacher Terri Fields puts the complaint process in a nutshell: "If you are not pleased with the answers you get, you can take further action. You can appeal the situation through the principal to the superintendent and then to the school board. If you are still unhappy, you may have legal recourse."

If you are interested in your specific rights as the parent of a child enrolled in the public school system, the National Committee for Citizens in Education (10840 Little Patuxent Parkway St. 301, Columbia, MD 21044-2396) will send you a list of your rights (include 29 cents for postage).

The old adage, "Use your brain before you use your mouth," is a good way to approach a conflict with school policy or personnel. Using the guidelines in this chapter and planning out a strategy, you'll solve your problem in an efficient and successful manner.

Parent and teacher communication

> "The basic fact for you to know in forming a partnership with a teacher for the best possible education of your child is simply this: Your goals are the same."
>
> — Mary Susan Miller, ***Bringing Learning Home***

Communication in person

Face-to-face contact with your child's teacher shows your child that you care about education, and shows the teacher that you care about your child. Scheduled meetings such as Back-to-school Night, conferences and Open House are important events that are worth the effort it may take to attend. Unscheduled contacts are very effective, but must be brief in consideration of the teacher's schedule.

Near the beginning of the year, it might be advantageous to make the teacher aware of your schedule with a remark such as the following:

> "I work full-time and won't be able to volunteer on a weekly basis. I value Caroline's education highly, so please let me know other ways that I can help."
>
> "With two little ones at home, it's hard for me to come to school. I'm fairly artistic, so if

> you have any drawing or lettering needs, please call me."
>
> "As a single dad, I'm spread pretty thin, but I would like to volunteer in the classroom one morning every month. Maybe I could tell the kids about my job as a paramedic."

Communication in writing

Notes are an effective and efficient method of communicating with your child's teacher (presuming you have a child who remembers to deliver them!). They are an appropriate way to handle minor issues or to set up a meeting to deal with a larger concern. Teachers generally prefer written communication because the teaching day is not disrupted and they are given time to think about the situation before responding. The teachers we surveyed emphasized the importance of keeping in touch through written notes.

Though most of your notes will concern specific school issues, an occasional note of appreciation gives a boost to a teacher's morale and motivation. Teachers keep special notes from students and their parents long after the gift coffee mugs have disappeared. The child is the beneficiary when the teacher knows that *you* appreciate her efforts.

Communication by phone

It is difficult to catch a teacher during a free moment, so in most instances she will be returning your call later in the day. Be sure to leave both your work and home phone numbers along with the reason for the call, unless it is confidential.

One teacher we surveyed advised parents to call and inform the teacher of any significant personal problems or developments their child may be having. Such a call helps a teacher stay abreast of any situations—from the birth of a sibling to the death of a grandparent—which might affect the child's behavior in the classroom. Call the teacher at school—it is not appropriate to call a teacher at home unless he or she has invited you to do so.

Communication via newsletter

One first-grade teacher asked parents to *"read and reread* newsletters sent home from the school." These are generally packed with information about school or classroom events. Put the upcoming events that you have an interest in directly on your calendar to remind yourself.

Communication of the future

> "In too many cases, schools blame parents for not coming to the school building. The parents feel guilty for not coming, and their children feel bad because their parents didn't participate. To reduce the guilt and distress, we need new ways of sharing information."
>
> — *Educational Leadership*

A high-tech system of school-to-home communication is being piloted in dozens of elementary schools across the country. These schools have purchased a computerized voice-mail system, which one school calls a "Parent Information Hotline." With a touch-tone phone, parents may listen to a prerecorded message from their child's teacher. Updated daily, the message focuses on classroom activities and homework assignments. Parents may push different buttons to access information about the PTA or school events. One principal, describing the popularity of his school's system adds, "Face-to-face contact is good. But for busy people, it may be a luxury they cannot afford."

Whether you are most comfortable communicating with your child's teacher in person, by phone or in writing, the important thing is to establish a *partnership.* Virginia Wimer, a veteran kindergarten teacher with 28 years of experience, sums it up this way: "Use every opportunity to talk with the teacher, not for long, but to *keep in touch."* Those last three words are the key to building this partnership.

Efficient parent conferences

Twenty minutes. It doesn't sound like much, but it's probably the longest block of time that you will spend one-on-one with your child's teacher. In elementary schools, scheduled conferences are usually held at the end of the first grading period, and perhaps again in the spring. At the junior-high level, conferences are held only by parent or teacher request because of the large number of students involved.

As a busy parent, you will need to take off time from work or get a baby sitter if you want to attend these conferences. Calling the school ahead of time may allow you to schedule appointments with all your children's teachers in consecutive time blocks (some schools do this automatically).

Having rearranged your whole day around the conference, you will certainly want to use those 20 minutes to their fullest. Here's how to get the most out of every conference.

Make a plan

Talk to your child before the conference. Is there anything he would like you to mention? Your son may tell you that he hates his seat because the boy behind him kicks him during class. Your daughter may confide that she gets a stomachache during math each morning. Think about the schoolwork that has been coming home. Consider your child's homework situation, and the ways in which you work with him during the afterschool hours.

Try to *get the whole picture,* then formulate a list of pertinent questions. When a teacher senses that a parent has made an effort to prepare for the conference, he or she is more motivated to make the meeting as productive as possible.

Arrive a few minutes early

If you're lucky, the teacher's previous meeting will have ended early and you'll be able to steal a few extra minutes. In any event, an early arrival will give you more preparation time.

If you are late, on the other hand, you will probably be frazzled and unable to think as clearly. In addition, the teacher will probably resent the disruption of her conference schedule.

Avoid small talk

Teachers are confused by parents who talk on and on about unrelated things during a conference. Are they trying to avoid discussing their child? Do they want to be friends? Are they in need of an ear to listen? Establishing a relationship with your child's teacher is extremely beneficial, but don't devote half of your conference to casual small talk.

Take notes

When your spouse asks, "So, what did Mrs. Blake say at the conference?" you may find that your mind is a blank. You will particularly want to remember the teacher's assessment of your child's strengths and weaknesses, and the ways in which you can best help him at home. In addition, it is important to give your *child* feedback about the conference. Reading him a few compliments from his teacher will be a boost to his self confidence at school.

Keep an eye on the clock

Every teacher has experienced a conference in which the parent brings up the major area of concern right before the scheduled end of the conference. The more complex the problem, the more likely the teacher is wondering how the heck she is going to discuss it in the minute or two left...knowing that the next parent is tapping her heels outside the classroom door.

Avoid putting your child's teacher in this awkward position by saying, "I still have some questions about Jim's reading. Perhaps we could continue the conference next week?"

Show appreciation

Your child's teacher may be talking to 15 or 20 parents on the day of your conference. The bright spot for him or her will be the parent who took the time to say, "Thanks so much for encouraging Sandy in math this year. He hated it before, but now it's his favorite subject."

Even if you're not thrilled with the teacher, try to think of one positive thing and say it.

Follow through

After discussing the conference with your child, you may want to make some alterations in your routine at home. Focus on the areas mentioned by the teacher, and use lists or charts as reminders for your child.

When there's a specific problem

In addition to regularly scheduled parent conferences, a teacher may call a parent and request a conference to discuss a problem that can't wait for the next conference. In ***Parent Conferences in the Schools,*** Stuart Losen and Bert Diament discuss parents reacting to negative information about their child: "At such times it is also not uncommon to find that the parents are experiencing overwhelming feelings of personal inadequacy and guilt in connection with the view that they have in some way failed their child."

Such a parent may be consumed by guilt but give an outward impression of defensiveness. It is never enjoyable to hear negative things about your child, but becoming defensive will make the meeting less productive and may alienate the very people who are trying to help your child.

Parents are not the only people who may become defensive in a conference, as Losen and Diament explain: "Staff members sometimes feel that they are on-the-spot to cover for a colleague or their own performance, or to vouch for a marginally supportable program or a questionable procedure. School personnel, by virtue of being public servants, have always been particularly vulnerable to public scrutiny, and in recent years the greater public demand for accountability has tended to increase their defensiveness."

Dissatisfaction with a particular school's or teacher's way of doing things is virtually inevitable during your child's school years. When it comes time to voice your displeasure, think before you speak. The teacher is as threatened by negative comments about her program as you are by negative findings about your child.

Approach the parent conference as an opportunity. Use the meeting to assess the way you use the precious minutes you spend working with your child. Plan ahead to make the conference productive, and then follow through at home. Making the best possible use of your time takes away the guilt you may feel because your time is limited.

Grades without guilt

Julie is going out to dinner with three close friends. She has looked forward to this "girls night out" for a month. Her husband, Rick, is home with their three children, aged 9, 3 and 1.

At dinner, the talk quickly turns to kids and school. One woman mentions casually that her third-grader brought his math grade up to an "A" after a month of nightly flash-card practice. Another mother laments the two hours she spends nightly on homework, adding, "but at least Karen got almost straight 'A's."

Julie sinks deeper into her chair. She had felt happy with her fourth-grader's report card—mostly "Bs", two "Cs", one "A." But after listening to her two friends, the results seem woefully inadequate.

"It's all my fault," Julie thinks. "I'm so busy with the younger kids that I don't spend enough time helping with schoolwork."

Julie ends the evening in a fog of guilt, feeling as though *she* earned less than excellent grades.

What are grades? And what do they really measure?

In ***How Was School Today, Dear?*** Sara Ann Friedman says, "If we are going to rely on a yardstick, let's not lose sight of what is supposed to be measured: learning." Unfortunately, many busy parents approach report cards with guilt and anxiety, feeling that their own self-worth is being evaluated.

In ***The National PTA Talks to Parents,*** Melitta Cutright implores parents to "remember that report cards are a measure of how students are doing in school, not of students' worth as individuals or of parents' success as parents."

Most teachers have witnessed at least one angry parent who marched into the principal's office because his or her child received all "As" and one "B+."

Who was *really* bothered and disappointed by the "B+"? Certainly not the student, who was probably embarrassed by his or her parent's behavior.

An overemphasis on grades gives children the wrong message. We need to be helpful and supportive of their learning, viewing grades as a measure of the past and a challenge for the future.

Finding the cause of poor grades

Given such a positive outlook, you must still be ready to confront the *causes* of very poor grades.

Your daughter slinks in the door, her report card in the very bottom of her backpack. One look at her face tells you that she doesn't have good news. Her report card reflects average and below-average grades.

What should you do?

Where do you begin?

First, consider her ***effort.*** Are assignments handed in late or not at all? Does she rush through her homework and have problems with neatness? If effort is the culprit, work together on a concrete plan for improvement.

Next, consider her ***ability.*** If her math grade has plummeted since she was moved up a level, perhaps it wasn't a good move. If spelling has always been a challenge, maybe it's time for a tutor. The teacher is your best resource in this area.

If neither effort nor ability appear to be a cause of low grades, a close look at your child's ***physical and emotional state*** may yield some clues. Perhaps repeated colds have caused her to fall far behind in her work. Maybe her reading difficulties are related to some undiagnosed vision problem. If her grades began to fall shortly after the new baby arrived, you may have your answer.

Make an effort to explore these possibilities rationally, without berating yourself and increasing your guilt. Your best insight in this area will come from talking to your child and seeing if the teacher has noticed recent changes at school.

Whether the problem appears to be related to effort, ability, or your child's physical or emotional state, determine a course of action and follow through. This will relieve your own guilt and stress while helping your child feel more secure.

In ***Making the Grade,*** Ginger Black encourages parents to react "candidly, casually and positively to their child's report card." Find areas of strength and give your child praise and encouragement. While a special dinner out to celebrate an academic achievement may be appropriate, beware of reward systems such as "five dollars for every 'A.'"

Studies by social psychologists indicate that such external rewards may actually decrease a child's internal motivation. In ***Education and the American Family,*** William Weston explains that "increasing internal motivation for school performance ought to be a central goal for parents and educators."

As a busy parent, you don't have unlimited hours to devote to your child's schoolwork. Use your child's grades as a focus of encouragement and motivation, rather than reward and punishment. This will give your child the best chance of developing an intrinsic desire to learn and achieve. Your guilt over grades will dissipate as your child becomes an independent learner who looks to you for guidance and support.

The time you take to learn about your children's school is an investment that will appreciate. It will allow you to maneuver efficiently within the system to meet your children's needs. Familiarity with the school system provides you with the confidence to communicate regularly and openly with school personnel.

Knowing that you are partners with your children's most vital allies erases the guilt that might be caused by "feeling out of touch."

Part Three

After-School Hours

Chapter Six

Reinforcing Academics at Home

Some experts will tell you that in order for your children to be successful you need to spend time teaching them to read, write and spell. We believe that teaching academic concepts is the *school's* responsibility. The *reinforcement* of those concepts is yours.

The next three chapters will show you how to reinforce academic success at home—without increasing your guilt or costing you hours of extra time you don't have anyway.

The big "H": Homework

What is homework supposed to do? In addition to strengthening school skills, homework teaches responsibility, autonomy, perseverance, time management and self-reliance. All of these skills are essential for a child to be successful at school.

In the old days—when fathers went off to work and mothers stayed home—there was more time for parents (especially moms) to assist their children with their homework. Interestingly enough, they didn't. This is not to say that 30 or 40 years ago people didn't work hard, because they did. The difference is that they didn't feel guilty for being busy.

Today, most parents recognize the basic principles of homework. These same parents, however, demonstrate different levels of involvement. Some parents with major time constraints are minimally involved and feel guilty. Others are motivated by guilt and over-compensate by being excessively involved in their kids' homework.

We advocate *moderate* involvement—reinforcing the teacher's homework goals by providing guidance with*out* taking on the responsibility yourselves. As teachers we spoke to put it, "Monitor and assist, but don't *do* it!"

Minimal involvement

Joey sits down at the kitchen table to do his homework as his mother begins to prepare dinner. He asks several questions. Mom keeps telling him to be quiet and study.

"Mom, can't you help me?" he asks.

"Not now," she answers. "I've got to get dinner cooked and the baby fed before your dad gets home. Plus I've got a meeting tonight."

Joey sits and daydreams and accomplishes very little.

"Joey, get that stuff off the kitchen table," Mom says. "Dinner will be ready in 20 minutes. Hurry and finish your homework."

Joey takes his homework into the living room and hurriedly writes a couple of sentences. He hasn't completed his math assignment. He puts it away anyway.

At dinner his mother asks, "Did you finish your homework?"

"Yeah," Joey answers. After all, it's the answer she wants to hear...whether or not it's true.

The mother in the above example is so busy and preoccupied that she is not involved in her son's homework at all. We realize that you may not have a big block of time to devote to monitoring your children's homework. However, time spent wisely today can save you time in the future.

When you are minimally involved in the homework process, the following situations occur:

1. Your child does not complete his or her work.
2. His or her teachers resent your lack of follow through.
3. Your child feels your lack of support.
4. You are unaware of what's going on in the classroom.

Maximum involvement

At a Back-to-school Night, a group of parents were standing outside a third-grade classroom waiting for the teacher to arrive. A conversation ensued:

> "I can't believe all the homework ***we*** have this semester."
>
> "Yeah, it's a lot more than last year."
>
> "My daughter not only has a contract with her spelling and math assignments, but ***we*** also have to write book reports and essays and poems."
>
> "It sure seems like a lot. I don't know how ***I'm*** going to find the time to do it all."

Parents may experience guilt when they don't spend as much time with their children as they think "good parents" should. So they overcompensate by helping *too* much. They also feel badly if their children's homework isn't done right, as if somehow it's a reflection on them—what will the teacher think *of them* if their children's homework isn't perfect?

Bill is an accountant and has had a very busy week. He had to work late every night and hasn't spent much time with his 11-year-old son, Jeremy.

"Have you completed your homework?" asks Bill.

"Some of it, but I haven't finished yet," says Jeremy, who is parked in front of the TV playing a video game.

Bill, who feels guilty for spending so little time on Jeremy's education, sees this as a great opportunity.

"Bring it here and let me see it," says Bill.

"Okay," says Jeremy, "but my math is too hard."

"You did the first five problems just fine. What about the rest?"

"They're harder."

Bill spends the next 20 minutes with Jeremy—doing his math problems for him. Next, Bill goes over a book report Jeremy has written.

"C'mon Jeremy, you can do better than this," says Bill. "You've misspelled five words, and it seems like you wrote this with your eyes closed. You didn't even explain what the book was about." Naturally, he then corrects the misspelled words and stands over Jeremy as he rewrites his report.

Bill, who has a very limited amount of time, wants desperately to make some significant contribution to his son's schooling. But by doing his son's homework rather than monitoring it, he's forgetting that homework is an opportunity for Jeremy to *learn and review.*

In our research, teachers and school administrators reported that homework should be a child's responsibility. One teacher said, "Children who are responsible for their own homework demonstrate a high degree of responsibility in other areas of their lives." They did however, stress that parents' attitudes toward homework and their willingness to help make a tremendous difference.

Parents who are too involved in homework tend to:

1. Prevent their child from learning from their mistakes.
2. Create anxiety by "hovering."
3. Assume the child's responsibility.
4. Encourage dependence rather than independence.
5. Send negative messages such as, "I don't think you're capable."
6. See their child's success or failure as their own.

Moderate involvement

A science fair was being sponsored by a local PTA. Three parents approached it quite differently.

One parent read about the project, felt that she had no time to help her child, and ignored the entire affair.

A second parent thought that it was a good opportunity to be active and helpful. She decided that she would help her child design a model of the solar system. On her way home from work on Friday, she picked up all the necessary supplies. She then spent the weekend hanging balls on a wire. Her child watched and helped a little but mostly played with her jump rope.

A third parent discussed the science fair with her son. They talked about different science questions. Her son, who had been learning about the five senses in school, asked his mom which sense was most important. She suggested he experiment and figure it out himself.

He got an apple, a potato and a radish. He then went to various family members, blindfolded them, had them plug their noses and ears, and told them to taste each item. When they couldn't decipher which was which, he concluded that you couldn't taste anything without the use of your other senses. He then wrote a simple report based on his findings.

The first child did not have an opportunity to enter the science fair at all and felt left out.

The second child won second place...and gave the ribbon to her mother—after all, *she* knew who really did the project.

The third child did not win anything, but he felt good about participating and accomplishing something on his own.

As a busy parent, your ultimate goal in homework involvement should be to help your child develop skills he or she needs to be a success. Parents who have only a few hours a week need to make sure that their time is used wisely. Moderate involvement helps you achieve that goal. It saves time, reduces guilt, and keeps the responsibility of homework projects and *learning* where it should be—with your *child*.

There are three potential areas of homework involvement—environment, structure and support. Here are some suggestions for how to maximize your contributions in each area.

Homework environment

1. Make sure your child has a quiet place to study and do homework. All necessary materials—pencils, erasers, dictionary, ruler, etc.—should be available. This special place should provide a child with

an environment in which he can accomplish what needs to be done *on his own.*

2. Wherever this "homework spot," the television should not be able to be seen or heard. Some children like to study while listening to music. Let your children do so if it does not distract them from the homework at hand.
3. Schedule homework time when you are home. If this is not possible, ask to see finished assignments every night.
4. Make sure your child has time to complete homework. If necessary, limit the amount of outside activities.

Homework structure

1. Establish a homework routine, scheduling "homework time" at the same time each day, if possible. Tell your child the minimum amount of time you expect him or her to spend studying each day. Whatever the particulars, your goal should be to encourage your child to make a habit of studying and completing homework.
2. Make sure your child understands your "homework rules." Go over these so there is no misunderstanding. A child who knows what's expected is less likely to break the rules.
3. Establish a homework schedule (teachers call it a contract) with your child. In lower grades, students are often provided

with a homework schedule. If yours are not, help them prepare a daily or weekly contract—it will help them learn organizational skills.

4. Set aside time to read with your child. If impossible to do this daily, don't waste time feeling guilty—plan and organize a time when you *can* do it.
5. Help your child organize finished assignments. A special folder in which to keep completed work will help avoid early morning hassles.
6. Go over your child's assignments. While it only takes a few minutes, teachers report that this lends significance to their work.

Homework support

1. Find out what is expected. Know the homework policy of the teacher. Ask about this at Back-to-school Night, a scheduled conference, or by phoning the teacher.
2. Praise your child for work well done. Always find something to compliment. Do not say, "This is good, but how come you missed that?" Focus on the positive.
3. Check the teacher's comments. On returned assignments, teachers will let you know what your child needs to work on, which will enhance the partnership between you and your children's teachers.
4. Maintain a positive attitude. Do not tell your child that you hated homework when you were

young. Or that homework is just busy work that needs to be done.

5. Show your child how valuable homework is. Attempt to apply homework to his or her daily life. One father we spoke with told his son about a man whom he interviewed for a position at his company. They were just about to hire him when the father reviewed his application—the applicant had misspelled several words. Since the job would have required him to write detailed reports, the man didn't get the job.
6. Find a convenient time to help. You'll only get frustrated if you try to help your child when you are busy or preoccupied.
7. Go over directions with your child. At times, your child may balk at this, saying he *knows* the directions, he just can't *follow* them. Going over a couple of examples will confirm whether your child understands the assignment.

And finally: ***Do Not Do Your Children's Homework!*** Remember, when you assist too much, teachers get false information about your child, perhaps thinking your child understands concepts he doesn't. It also sends a message to your child—that you believe he can't accomplish things on his own. This can poke a pretty big hole in your child's self-esteem.

Neither minimum nor maximum involvement helps your child reach his potential. Being *moderately* involved in your child's homework teaches him to think for himself and be responsible. Any child who acquires these skills is well on his way to becoming a successful student.

Moderate involvement also enables you to stay in touch with what your child is studying, and gives you an excellent opportunity to be involved in his education.

Finding time for each child

It's a bright sunny afternoon. Linda has taken her children to the park, where she meets Kelly, who has her own two kids in tow.

"I can't believe it's been so long since I've gotten a chance to bring the kids to the park," says Linda, watching Mark, 7, Nicole, 5, and Kevin, 3, attack the jungle gym.

"I know. I used to be such a good mom," sighs Kelly. "When Katie was a baby, I took her all over the place. With the new baby, I don't seem to have any extra time."

"I know what you mean," says Linda. "When Mark was a baby, I would talk to him and read to him all the time. Then Nicole came along, and I didn't spend as much time with her. Now Kevin. Poor Kevin, he just has to fend for himself. I feel so guilty, but I have so little time."

Some variation of this conversation goes on daily between parents who feel they are neglecting their younger children due to a lack of time. Is it any wonder that the second, third, or fourth child survives at all? Of course, they *do*...and they usually do quite well, thank you, *despite the guilt we feel.*

Reality: With each additional child, the amount of work we have multiplies. We have less time to spend with each child. Feeling guilty about that fact does not change it. This problem is only compounded when our kids enter the school system. Avoiding over-involvement and burnout is particularly important when you have more than one child. Being able to balance your life and organize your time so that each child benefits from your participation is crucial.

A few years ago, Linda used to volunteer in her oldest son's class every week and make special art projects for his teacher. Now she is working part-time and still volunteering, but not as much. With her third child, she's finding she has even less time. She cannot keep up this pace. There is just not enough time.

She *can* maintain a level of involvement and commitment to education without feeling guilty or neglectful.

Each one of your children deserves some time with you. And certainly you want to spend quality time with each of your children and be involved in such a way that you help them achieve success. The fact is, you will not be able to spend as much time with subsequent children as you did with the first. Time, responsibilities, and commitments will not allow it.

The second child in the family who is read to 15 minutes a day doesn't feel badly because his older sister was read to 45 minutes a day. The only person who feels badly is the *parent,* who wastes time feeling guilty because he thinks he should be doing for his younger child exactly what he did for the older one.

Stop feeling guilty. Your second child will benefit from your involvement just as much as your first *even though the amount of time you spend with each is not the same.* The second child is also the beneficiary of your older child's experience, which, to some extent, replaces the time you have to spend with him or her.

Busy parents must remember that it is not the *amount* of time you spend with each child, but *how* you spend that precious time. Here are some suggestions:

- Plan a special date with one child. This can be as infrequently as once a month and does not have to be something elaborate—a ride for ice cream qualifies.
- Depending on your particular time constraints, plan to spend 5, 10 or 15 minutes

with just one child. This does not have to be done daily. How you allocate these blocks of time depends on the age of the child—younger children will undoubtedly demand more of your time.

- If you volunteer in the classroom, alternate time spent between each of your children's classes.
- Whenever possible, combine activities so that they involve all of your children. A mother who is setting dinner on the table may ask her 2-year-old, "I just poured something in this glass. What is it?" "Milk," he answers. "What letter does 'milk' start with?" she asks her 4-year-old. "M," she replies. "Okay," says Mom to her 6-year-old, "How do you spell it?"

  All the kids are participating and Mom has successfully made a contribution to each of her kids in only a few seconds.
- A positive comment to each child every night makes each feel important: "I liked the drawing you made today." "I appreciated your putting your bike away." "I'm glad you did such a nice job on your math homework." These statements—accompanied by a hug and a kiss goodnight—make each child feel appreciated and special.

A child remembers precious moments that are meaningful and sincere. The few minutes you devote gives each child a sense of confidence and worth, feelings that carry over to his or her school performance.

In the following section, we describe a number of activities and games that will help you enhance your children's learning and enable you to include each of them.

Quick learning games and activities

The recent trend in education—emphasizing the parent/teacher partnership—is not intended to make parents feel as if they have to add "educator" to their growing list of parental responsibilities. The basic aim of this partnership is for parents to *assist* and *support*. Guilt should not be a force that drives you to spend hours in an educational resource center or a children's bookstore searching for activities and special projects to help your child learn. It *is* possible to support education, encourage your child's efforts, and reinforce the teacher's goals without spending a lot of time or a lot of money.

There are a variety of activities that can be done at home, in the car, or out in the community which can assist your child in a variety of academic areas. Let's first look at some games that teach necessary skills that every child needs to be successful in school.

For Younger Children

Memory
Candyland
Chutes & Ladders
Bingo games

These games teach numbers, colors and sequences. They help a child learn to concentrate, to follow rules, to share, and to take turns—all essential skills.

For any game, you can set a time limit and declare whoever is ahead when time runs out the winner.

For older children

Clue
Monopoly
Sorry
Checkers
Fish
Old Maid

These games teach strategy, sportsmanship and money management.

Any time you sit and play a game with your child, you are involving yourself in his or her education. You are reinforcing what's being taught in school, spending quality time—even if there are disagreements during the game—and helping him or her practice listening skills.

The following are specific activities that can help build your child's academic skills in a variety of areas. Your child can be doing them even while you are busy doing other things.

Math

- Turn various household chores into math games. Have your children count out four forks, four knives and four spoons, then tell you how many total pieces there are. While doing laundry, have them sort by color, then add up the number of clothes by color.

- Cut bread, lunch meat and cheese for sandwiches in different shapes, then have the child match them.
- In the car, have your child count how many trucks he sees. You can do it by color, cars vs. trucks vs. motorcycles, etc.
- Practice fractions while folding clothes in half or quarters. Cut pizza or a piece of cheese in pieces and have them figure out how many it takes to make a whole.
- If you have a scale, practice estimating by having a child guess the weight of an object and then checking it on the scale.
- Have an older child guess how much all the grocery items you've bought will cost, then check it with the actual receipt.

Language arts

- Ask your child to find a particular letter on any number of items in the house (cans of food, cereal boxes, cleaning supplies, etc.).
- Read as often as possible. Reread books—have your child finish the sentence while you point to the word.
- Play rhyming games.
- Tell a story and have your child make up his own ending.
- Write a simple note—e.g., "I love you." As your child gets older, write more complex notes. When your child begins writing, ask questions verbally, but then have your

child respond in writing: What would you like to do on Saturday? Tell me one thing you liked about school today.
- Play 20 questions—"I'm thinking of something in the kitchen that starts with the letter 'S' (stove, sink, salad). What is it?"
- As your child gets older, have him or her read a recipe for you or read a story to you while you're preparing dinner.

Science

- Enhance your children's observational and questioning skills by encouraging them to ask questions and discover answers.
- Place a dish of water outside on a hot day. As it disappears, your children will learn about evaporation.
- Teach your children about cause and effect by taking two small plants and putting one in the closet, the other on a sunny shelf. Ask them what they think will happen and why.

Social studies

- Make outings a learning experience. When you eat out, occasionally choose an ethnic restaurant and discuss the cultural differences (food, clothing, customs).
- On trips, point out places on a map and discuss geographical differences, seasons and weather.
- Teach your children about the community and careers. In the grocery store, ask your children

how they think the groceries got on the shelf. Where does the food come from, and who brings it to the store? In the post office, ask how the letter gets from one place to another.

These activities take very little time and can easily be incorporated into your daily routines. They provide a positive component to the home/school partnership. And everyone gets something out of it!

Your child's teacher benefits as you reinforce what's being taught in the classroom.

Your child benefits because you are demonstrating your interest in learning and participating in the process.

And you benefit because you know your involvement is valuable and that you're using your time wisely.

Just for dads

Frank is an attorney with two kids, Adam, 11, and Amy, 7. He works long hours, rarely coming home before 6:30 pm. He tries to be home for dinner at least three or four nights a week, but usually only makes it one or two. He also tries to spend time on the weekends with the kids, though he often has to go into the office for a few extra hours.

This past weekend, Frank had an opportunity to take Adam camping overnight with their local Indian Guide Troop. After all the boys were safely tucked in, Frank and Charlie, another father with two kids, had a chance to talk:

"You know, I love these weekends when I can spend some time alone with Adam, but do you ever feel pressured to do more?" asks Frank.

"All the time," answers Charlie. "The old days must have been great. My dad used to come home from a lolg day, pop open a beer, and sit in his chair until dinner was on the table. When he came home from work, his day was over. With my wife working part-time, I've got a lot more to do."

"Yeah," says Frank. "I know what you mean. We got a note from Adam's teacher saying he's not doing as well as he could. My wife says I've got to help Adam more, especially since she started teaching two nights a week. It's not that I don't want to help. I mean, I care about the kids as much as she does. I just don't know how to squeeze it all in. Plus I'm not sure *how* to help him."

Fathers today feel pressure like never before. In the past, a father's role was clearly defined, and it had been similarly structured for decades. Today's fathers are being asked to be involved in ways *their* fathers and grandfathers never were. With more and more women working outside the home and living more complex lives, many men find themselves experiencing guilt as they struggle to juggle the demands of parenthood.

Due to their busy schedules, today's mothers are pressuring their spouses to take a more active role. They are saying that the schools want parent involvement and that means not just *me* but *you,* too! Fathers are now being placed in situations where they have to balance their time. They are struggling with what they *should* do vs. what they *can* do and *want* to do.

Certainly most of the ideas for being efficiently involved in your child's education throughout this book are just as applicable to fathers as mothers. Here are some suggestions just for busy fathers:

- A dad who assists with chores around the house teaches his children cooperation, a skill essential for school success. When a father takes some responsibility, a child learns the importance of each family member doing his or her share.

- The teachers in our research said the most effective way for busy fathers to be involved was to *show interest and support* at every opportunity, no matter how rare. Finding out about special events at the beginning of the school year helps a father plan to attend the most important functions.
- A father who is playing and having fun with his kids is contributing to their education. Finding a few minutes to play with your kids makes them feel special, enhances self-esteem, and gives you an opportunity to communicate and listen. These are all valuable ways to be involved.
- If you work long hours, be selective. Do not attempt to do more than you can.
- Sometimes it's necessary to pack a lot into a short amount of time. One father, an accountant with four children, has an exceptionally busy three months at the beginning of each year. Once a week he comes home early, plays with his three boys, then picks up his daughter at an after-school activity. They go to a local pizza pub and discuss school activities. When he returns home, he goes over their homework and reads them a story. The rest of his week is pretty full, but on weekends he goes over the week's homework with each child and offers positive comments and encouragement.

- By setting a good example, a father increases his chances of sending a child to school who will behave appropriately.
- A father can show how much he values his child's work by hanging up artwork or writing assignments in his office or place of business.
- Establishing rituals involves little time and is a great way to maintain involvement. Once a month, one father who owns his own business and leaves early every morning takes his kids to school. Another father who cannot take time off during school hours makes pancakes for his kids every weekend. While he fixes breakfast, he runs a spelling bee for his two kids.
- Divorced fathers can also be actively involved without feeling guilty or left out. If your school has a "homework hotline," use it. If not, contact the teacher and ask him or her to send you a classroom newsletter. When kids see that Dad knows what's going on and is interested, their attitude will reflect that interest.

Reinforcing "value" units

Schools are now teaching subjects that go beyond basic academics—classes on health and environmental issues, sex education, drug awareness, AIDS, self esteem and more.

Most busy parents appreciate the effort teachers are putting forth helping their children understand these complex issues. Teachers, on the other hand, need to know these efforts are supported and that parents are actively involved. A child benefits the most from his or her school experience when whatever is taught or discussed in class is reinforced in the home.

When value-laden units are being introduced into the classroom curriculum, children bring home written information for parents to view. The following ideas will help you reinforce that curriculum:

- Take the time to go over the issues. This is an excellent opportunity to find out how your child feels about these subjects.
- Discuss possible problems and solutions. Children need an opportunity to discuss their views and their thoughts on a variety of issues. Parents who listen encourage their children's curiosity and promote problem solving abilities.
- Practice good standards at home. A child whose family recycles is already practicing the child's environmental class is "preaching."
- Don't take drugs or drink excessively. Today, even kids in kindergarten are taught about the dangers of drug abuse. If what they are learning in school is completely contradicted by what they see at home, the teacher feels undermined and not supported. Like it or not, kids model our behavior. So set a good example.

A few minutes is all it takes. Riding in the car, at the dinner table, or at bedtime is a great time to discuss sensitive issues. It's also a perfect time to reinforce your own family values. Having family discussions and practicing good listening skills sets the tone for how your child will communicate with you as the formidable "teen years" approach.

Taking the time to allow your children to express their views and opinions is extremely important for them to mature and develop their independence. Yes, it takes a little bit of time, but it will undoubtedly pay off down the line. It can also prevent a parent's guilt in the future.

We hope you never have to look back on your child's early years and say, "I wish I'd taken the time to talk about this when they were younger."

Chapter Seven

Time Crunch of Extracurricular Activities

What kind of future do you dream for *your* children?

What do you hope they will become? Do you want them to follow in your footsteps and match or exceed your accomplishments? To aspire to something that you always wanted to do but lacked the time or talent or drive to achieve? To be a world-famous scientist, a prize-winning novelist, a respected teacher or social worker or lawyer or doctor or...?

Whatever the specifics, we all occasionally wonder just what our children will become, dream of what we would *like* them to be, and try to spur them on to be the best they *can* be. Sometimes that drive helps our kids, and sometimes it is a hindrance.

As your child begins participating in extracurricular experiences—with or without your encouragement or help—remember that *he or she is not you.* Let your child dream his own dreams, not yours. By helping him choose the activities that are best for him—by backing him up without pushing too hard—you will allow him to reap the physical, social and cultural benefits of involvement.

Moderation is key

Nine-year-old Alex stares wistfully out his bedroom window. "Can I just go outside and play with the guys for 10 minutes, Mom?"

Alex's mother, Andrea, is changing the baby and dressing her two year old. "No Alex, I told you to get your towel and get ready for swimming lessons. Hurry, we need to leave in five minutes!"

"But Mom, we have swimming on Monday, Wednesday and Friday, art lessons on Tuesday, and a baseball game every Thursday. I never get to go out and ride bikes with my friends."

Susan swallows the guilt that Alex's complaint elicits and tries to diffuse his frustration. "You do have less playtime, Alex, but look how much you're learning and how well you're doing. You're one of the fastest nine year olds at swimming, your drawing gets better every week, and last Thursday you caught a fly ball that was way over your head. You told me that when the kids play baseball at recess, they always pick you first. Doesn't that make you feel great?"

"Well, yeah, it makes me feel okay, but sometimes I just feel like sitting around after school instead of going somewhere everyday."

"Once you get in the water you'll be fine. Get your towel, we need to leave now."

Sam sits on his bike and watches as his friend Alex leaves for swimming lessons. When his mother gets home from work at 4:30, Sam meets her at the car. "Mom, why can't I do any of the neat stuff that Alex does after school?"

Susan sighs. She is exhausted from a busy day at work and doesn't feel ready for this discussion. "Sam, all of those things take too much time and too much money. Besides, you have lots of fun playing outside with the other kids on the street. Alex probably wishes he could play outside more."

"Yeah, but Alex is really good at a lot of stuff like drawing and baseball, and sometimes at recess the guys who play on the baseball team don't let the other guys in the game."

"Let's talk about this later, Sam. Will you please help me carry my things into the house?"

Andrea and Alex are having a problem, and so are Susan and Sam. Both mothers feel very guilty. Andrea, secure that she is helping Alex develop valuable skills, nevertheless feels guilty about pushing him so hard. And Susan, happy that Sam has ample time to play and relax, feels guilty that Sam is not being exposed to new experiences.

Andrea worries that Alex will burn out on swimming, his strongest sport. Susan gets a sinking feeling in her stomach when she realizes that Sam can't throw and catch as well as the other kids.

What should Andrea and Susan do?

Aim for the middle! As in most things, moderation is often the best route to take with extracurricular activities.

As a busy parent, you have a limited amount of time to devote to your child's extracurricular activities. Opportunities are almost endless: the arts—including dance, music, studio art and drama—team sports, individual sports, religious and church-related activities, and many others. By selectively choosing one or two extracurricular activities at a time, you will be exposing your child to new experiences and new friends without filling every waking moment with a structured activity. How do you decide? Here are some questions to ask yourself:

1. What would your child ***like*** to do?
2. What are his present ***skills and abilities?***
3. Would it be best for your child to ***develop*** those skills further or to try a ***new*** activity?
4. What activities do you enjoy doing ***with your child?***
5. How much ***parental time*** does the activity entail?
6. Does the activity fit into your ***schedule and budget?***

Once you and your child have decided on an activity, it is important to support his or her efforts. In ***The Sports-Confident Child,*** Chris Hopper says, "The basis of the parent-child partnership is adults' understanding of and preparation for all the different aspects of their child's involvement. By partnership I don't mean the type where the parent stands on the sideline and screams, telling their child when to move and how fast. Rather, adults must work toward a supportive partnership where they and their child...set goals for the personal growth of the child."

Providing this support for your child can be difficult when you are a busy or working parent. By limiting the number and extent of your child's outside activities to those you can handle, and working cooperatively with other parents, you will be able to offer your support.

Being selective about your child's extracurricular activities means that you will have enough time to support his or her efforts. You will also be free of the guilt generated when your child is either uninvolved or over-involved.

Striving for ***balance*** will help you and your child make smart choices.

Benefits of physical activity

When our children are physically active, they reap benefits in many different areas. With consistent activity, our children discover that their bodies feel better, function better, even look better. They are stronger, healthier, more alert and more confident.

For busy parents, finding time in their children's schedule for exercise may well be a challenge. But it is a challenge worth meeting, since the alternative is a sedentary child and a guilty parent. Here are some simple ways to meet that challenge:

Structured activities

Soccer, swimming, basketball, dance, tennis, volleyball, gymnastics and a multitude of other activities are available to your child. Check these sources to find out what structured activities are offered in your area: flyers sent home from school, the PTA newsletter, the local newspaper, the city parks and recreation guide. Kids who might otherwise resist playing outside will grab their cleats when it's time for soccer practice.

The discipline of organized sports is easily applied to the school situation, developing such skills as respecting authority and meeting a tough challenge. And best of all, as your kids enjoy the company of their friends and concentrate on learning new skills, they'll be developing a higher level of fitness.

Unstructured playtime

If putting your child on an organized team or in a structured lesson is not feasible due to time, expense or simply personal preference, you need not feel guilty about your child's level of activity. By channeling his free time into outdoor activities, you can ensure that he gets adequate exercise. Encourage him to ride his bike, jump rope, play tag, chase, hide and seek, and, of course, games like basketball and soccer. Keeping the TV off is a good way to encourage kids to go out and play.

Moms, dads and kids

One of the best ways to teach your kids about fitness is by example. Kids adore doing something physical with their mother or father. For the busy parent, this may take some creativity. When time permits, the following are great ways to include your child:

> "Would you like to run around the block with me before I go for my jog?"
>
> "I'm going to do some exercises to this aerobics tape. I'll teach you some—just copy what I do."
>
> "Let's kick the soccer ball around while we're waiting for Dad to get home."
>
> "Mom and I are going to play tennis. Why don't you bring your racket along, and we'll hit you some balls."

Whether your child is raising her heart rate by playing on a soccer team, chasing the kid next door, or bike riding next to you, her body is attaining a higher level of fitness. Consistent exercise benefits her body in many ways:

The way the body functions

Daily exercise actually changes the way in which your child's body functions. The body works more efficiently as your child builds up his cardiovascular endurance. Other areas such as muscle strength, agility and flexibility also improve, depending on the nature of the activity.

In ***The Well Child Book,*** Mike and Nancy Samuels describe some of these changes: "When kids exercise rather than sit still, their bodies work very differently. Their heart pumps faster, sending out more than four times as much blood. Their breathing speeds up and their lungs take in 20 times as much air. And their blood vessels widen in the big muscles, bringing in 20 times as much blood. The more kids exercise, the bigger and stronger their heart, lungs, blood vessels and muscles..."

The way the body feels

You are having a busy and stressful week at work. Working late a few times has made it impossible to get to your aerobics class, and even taking a walk around the block during a coffee break has been out of the question. You meant to get up early and ride the exercycle at home, but the snooze button was just too tempting. As the week ends, you notice that you have felt sluggish at work, cranky with the kids, and unable to fall asleep at night. Feeling guilty about your lack of activity, you make a commitment to exercise next week...no matter what.

As adults, we know that exercise can affect our whole outlook on life. The same is true for our children. Kids who have been inactive during the day have pent up energy, energy that may be released in negative ways at home or at school. Kids who get little or no exercise do not concentrate as well at school and tend to have poorer attendance.

Regular exercise helps a child fall asleep more easily at night and wake up refreshed in the morning. A rested child is healthier and more responsive to learning.

The way the body looks

A child's body image permeates his or her whole personality. The importance of this seems to reach a peak in junior high school, when almost every adolescent feels dissatisfied with his or her body. Regular exercise alters the appearance of the body in a positive way—reducing excess body fat and toning muscles. These changes result in a higher level of self-confidence, which leads to success in school.

By being aware of your child's activity level, you can ensure that he gets an adequate amount of exercise. Between structured sports, informal playtime and active time with you, exercise can be squeezed into even the busiest schedule. Making exercise a priority for your child means that he will enjoy the benefits of a fit body that functions smoothly and feels well. The self confidence that will become a part of his personality will erase your guilt and spur you on to be a physically fit parent!

The fatigue factor

Tina is thinking about a morning sales meeting as she rushes to put on her makeup. Her daughter, Stacy, is finishing a bowl of cereal. "Hurry up, Stacy," Tina yells. "The bus will be here in five minutes!"

Stacy looks up at her mother and bursts into tears. "I don't want to go to school, Mom. I'm too tired."

Tina groans inwardly. If Stacy misses the bus and needs a ride to school, she will be late for her meeting. "But, honey," Tina says, "you went to bed at the usual time."

"I know I did," Stacy answers. "But going to swim practice every day makes me too tired!" Stacy pushes her cereal bowl aside, puts her head on the kitchen table, and sobs.

Tina sighs as she walks to the telephone to call her boss.

Tina has mixed emotions. She feels confident that she has taken the time to expose Stacy to outside activities, and she is proud of her daughter's swimming skills and fitness level. On the other hand, she is seeing frequent examples of Stacy's fatigue, and each one generates more parental guilt. What should Tina do?

Tina can strive for more balance in her daughter's schedule in a number of ways. Perhaps Stacy's coach would allow her to change her workouts to three days a week instead of four. Tina could also try to plan quiet, restful activities for the days that Stacy doesn't swim. Maybe Stacy's bedtime could be moved up. Perhaps it's even time to stop swimming for a few months.

Being attuned to the signs of fatigue can make your child's extracurricular involvement beneficial rather than detrimental. Fatigue can manifest itself in many ways. Children highly involved in activities, particularly sports, may demonstrate ***general fatigue, overuse injuries*** or ***burn-out.*** Each of these situations generates guilt and distress in parents. Fortunately, each one can be avoided.

General fatigue

When the balance in a child's day is tipped toward over-involvement in activities, general fatigue is the result. The child may be listless, sluggish and overly sensitive. Continual fatigue breaks down the immune system and leads to more colds and viruses.

A tired child has a difficult time paying attention and absorbing information. Teachers get frustrated with the parents of students who are continually overtired.

If you have overcommitted your child's time, stop feeling guilty and do something about it. The pain of quitting an activity you have already paid for will disappear as your child becomes a happier, more alert person.

Overuse injuries

Shelley plays soccer in the fall, basketball in the winter, and softball in the spring. When she doesn't have practice, she loves to ride her bike all over the neighborhood. Shelley is probably not a candidate for an overuse injury, however, because her sports are so varied.

Jason is 10 years old and dreams of being a major league pitcher. Though Little League limits the innings he can pitch, he practices incessantly at home with his father and goes to specialized training programs every summer. Jason is a prime candi-date for elbow problems.

Dr. John Harvey of the Fort Collins Sports Medicine Clinic explains that "hours of practicing the same movements produce gradual wear and tear on specific parts of the body." In ***The Sports-Confident Child,*** Chris Hopper describes how trauma to the growth centers of the bones of young athletes can cause "a permanent growth disturbance."

Help your child avoid an overuse injury by being sure that he or she warms up properly and limits highly repetitive motions.

Burn-out

Kids who are involved in sports for the joy of playing and competing are the least likely candidates for burn-out. When the intensity of practice and competition, however, mounts to the point that it ceases to be fun for the young athlete, burn-out begins. Many victims of burn-out have been pushed too hard for too long. Former pro tennis player Arthur Ashe asserts that "if a child is playing to please his parents, he is playing for the wrong reasons."

Sports psychologist Dr. Bruce Ogilvie warns about being vicariously involved in your child's athletic achievements: "As the child progresses, the involvement gets more intense and the parents grow increasingly neurotic. This neurosis takes many forms. The most prevalent is the parent who for whatever reason is dissatisfied with his or her own life and climbs right into the child's bloodstream until it is no longer the child's activity."

If your child is exhibiting anxiety, negativism or a loss of interest regarding his sport, he may be feeling too much pressure from you, his coach or himself. This pressure can manifest itself in the classroom, leaving your child with little energy for academics. Help him to reduce or eliminate this stress. You will increase his fun and avoid burn-out in the process.

As a busy parent, you probably find your own schedule hectic and tiring. Don't plan the same schedule for your kids! When all of their playtime is highly structured, it begins to seem like work. Be aware of the signs of mental and physical fatigue, and be flexible enough to reduce their activities as needed.

Social benefits of involvement

Robert is 8 years old, an average student who poses no problems at school or at home. His mother and father both work and don't arrive home until 5:30 pm. His older sister Kate, 13, makes sure Robert does his homework, then they both watch TV until Mom and Dad come home.

At first glance, it would seem as if Robert and Kate are just fine. At school, however, they usually play by themselves. They are somewhat shy and reserved, and during group activities are often reluctant to participate.

Learning for a child does not end at the close of school. Benefits from after-school involvement transfer into the classroom and help a child in a variety of activities. Children are often asked tm work on projects in a group or to perform tasks that require special social skills. Any and all after-school activities afford a child the opportunity to develop these talents.

In the previous section, we discussed the physical benefits of after-school activity. There are also social benefits which should not be overlooked.

1. After-school activities are ***fun.*** Finding an activity that your kids like and enjoy can bring a smile to their faces. A youngster should not spend an inordinate amount of time under pressure to achieve. A child who has time to *have fun* goes to school with a smile and is energized and motivated to learn.
2. After-school activities allow a child to socialize and ***meet new friends.*** Every school year a child is put into a new situation with new people. A child who has learned to adapt to new situations *out* of school can use that skill *in* school.
3. Whether a child is involved in organized sports, such as soccer or gymnastics, belongs to a community theater group, or is taking swimming lessons, he learns ***cooperative behavior.*** During these activities, a child needs to practice listening, following rules, and taking turns. When your child enjoys the activity he is involved in, he cooperates without much effort. He also learns the benefits cooperation bestows, an attitude that carries over into the school environment.
4. Many times ***sportsmanship*** is a big part of after-school activities. It is not always easy for a child

to learn to be a good sport, especially in the competitive world in which we live. Because of that competition, it is extremely important that a child learn how to win as well as lose, how to succeed as well as fail, and how to accept situations where he or she has no control. A child who plays the best baseball game of her life, but whose team loses anyway, needs skills to cope with her disappointment. The same is true for a young pianist who comes in second in an important competition. A child learns flexibility and adaptability through mastering skills and becoming a good sport.

5. Lastly, after-school activities can boost a child's ***self esteem*** and ***confidence***. This can only be accomplished when there is not an excess amount of parental pressure.

A busy parent should not be motivated by guilt to enroll his or her child in every available after-school activity—we've already discussed the negative implications of such over-involvement. Instead, watch and listen. Once you've identified specific areas of interest to your child, find an activity or two that will encourage that interest.

Cultural enrichment

By the time Britany was 8 years old, she had been to three foreign countries, visited several museums and art galleries, attended the opera and ballet, and cruised the Mediterranean. Has Britany benefited more than someone who has not had these experiences? Not necessarily! In fact, probably not!

Cultural enrichment can take many forms. It does not mean you must expend a great amount of time and expense in order to bring culture into your child's life. Cultural enrichment—enhancing our child's interest in the arts—can be accomplished with very little time, very little money, and very little extra effort. For example:

1. If your child is studying about Native Americans in school, take a few minutes in the library to look at some pictures of Indian art. Discuss each picture and how it was done. What materials and tools did they use and why?
2. During dinner at an ethnic restaurant, discuss the cultural differences between the U.S. and that country. For example, in a Chinese restaurant, ask your child why they cook their food in a wok. Why do they use chopsticks? And where *is* China, anyway?
3. Listen to a variety of music in your home. Talk about the regional and ethnic differences between different kinds of music and different artists. Help your children decipher the various instruments used and gain an appreciation and greater understanding of various musical forms.

When time permits, you can integrate cultural activities into your child's life. Here are a few ways to do so:

1. Visit the library.
2. See a play. Many communities have local theater groups.
3. Rent a travel film.
4. Plan a trip to a museum. (Just don't try to take in too much. A children's museum is a good start.)

5. Attend music festivals featuring different musical styles. Many of these are free to the public.

You can expose your children to a wide range of culture without spending hours in the process. But avoid "overexposing" your child. Busy parents often ease the guilt they feel if they're away from home too much by overindulging in activities and events when they are home.

A child who is exposed to all the culture in the world, but has not had very much of his or her parents' undivided attention, is *not* richer for the experience.

Chapter Eight

The "Guilt Box" All About Television

As part of our research, we asked educators to grade parents on different aspects of childrearing. The grade in one area stood out: A remarkable *71 percent of educators gave parents a grade of either "D" or "F" on "using television appropriately."* These educators are seeing the effects of uncontrolled TV watching in the classroom... and don't like what they're seeing.

Unless you have pulled the plug on your television, it is having an impact on how and what your child is learning. The role that television plays in your household determines whether that impact is positive or negative.

Does the scope of television enrich your child's knowledge?

Or are hours and hours of unrestricted viewing sending your child's school performance downward?

Most of us with young children have a love/hate relationship with our television sets. We use TV to gain extra time, letting it "watch" and entertain our children. Then, even as we accomplish what we need to do, we feel guilty for using the television as an "electronic babysitter."

This chapter is devoted to the efficient and appropriate use of television. With a small amount of effort, you *can* turn your "guilt box" into a source of learning and family enrichment.

"Can we watch TV, Daddy?" asks 7-year-old Courtney in her sweetest voice. "Please?" adds 5-year-old Michael. "There's nothing else to do!"

Jerry sighs. He wishes Linda didn't work on Saturday mornings, but the extra money comes in handy. On her way out the door this morning she had said, "Have fun playing with the kids!"

I shouldn't just let them watch television, Jerry thinks to himself. On the other hand, I need to mow the lawn and get an hour or so of paperwork done. "Okay kids," Jerry says. "I guess you can watch a little television while I do some of my work."

Courtney and Michael sit mesmerized in front of the set, watching cartoon after cartoon. They shout with glee at the commercials for sugary cereals and plastic guns.

Jerry's guilt mounts as the morning passes by. He feels torn between the need to complete his work and his desire to spend time with his children. The lawn takes longer to mow than usual, and the paperwork hits several snags. Time passes quickly, and suddenly it's time for Linda to come home.

Jerry turns off his computer as Linda comes in the back door. "Hi kids. What did you and Daddy do this morning?" They quickly tell her.

Linda glares at Jerry as he enters the kitchen. "I thought you were going to do something fun with the kids," she says in an accusing tone.

Jerry's guilt turns into defensiveness. "I can't do everything at once! I did the yard and finished some work that I brought home from the office. What do you want me to do?"

Jerry and Linda table their heated discussion for the sake of Courtney and Michael, though, of course, it will come up again...tomorrow morning. Jerry scowls at the television set as he stalks through the family room. "We should just unplug you," he mutters.

Moderate use without guilt

> "In America, the television has become a member of the family that has to be dealt with like any other member...We'd like to see people take advantage of this new member of the family, and encourage it to be disciplined."
>
> — Elizabeth Thoman, Executive Director
> USC Center for Media and Values

Most experts recommend that children watch no more than two hours of television per day; many feel that one hour should be the maximum allowed on school days. Meanwhile, the average child in elementary school watches 25 hours of television a week.

What is the amount of television appropriate for your family? If you feel it's far less than they're watching now, how do you alter their behavior?

Children who are accustomed to watching a great deal of television may complain of boredom when their viewing is limited. Dr. William Dietz, spokesperson for the American Academy of Pediatrics, explains that "children don't need to be doing something constantly. One of the most powerful forces for the development of self-reliance and creativity is boredom." Most kids just need a nudge in the right direction. When you turn off the TV and hand the average 8-year-old a blanket, he'll spend the next half hour making a tent and "camping."

Being in control of your television set necessitates making some TV rules. *NEA Today*, a journal for educators, describes an informal study done by a third-grade teacher. The teacher found that her students who read above grade level had rather strict TV rules, such as "I have to ask permission to watch TV." Her grade-level readers had moderate rules like "I can't watch TV until I finish my homework." The below grade-level readers had few, if any, rules. As one child put it, "I watch TV whenever I want."

Only you can determine the TV rules appropriate for your family. The amount of control you can exert depends upon your personality and the ages of your children. If you are determined to make some changes, here are some rules you might want to incorporate into your TV limits:

- No more than _____ hour(s) of TV per day.
- Homework must be completed before the TV goes on.
- No random viewing, ask permission first.
- Pick shows in advance, then turn the TV on at the beginning of the show, off at the end.
- Add your own limits for video games like Nintendo.
- Encourage public television—try giving your kids the choice of one "regular" show or *two* shows from public television.
- Establish rules for viewing if your child is home alone.

Establishing reasonable limits on television viewing will decrease your guilt regarding the TV. The next step is to become aware of harmful TV patterns, and actively avoid them.

Patterns to avoid

Sometimes television becomes so entrenched in a child's life that even an outside observer—his teacher—is aware of it's influence. If you see your child's personality being shaped by this electronic force, it's time to make some changes in the role of television in your household. Here are five examples of the way kids' personalities can reflect their television-viewing habits.

The hermit

Why is Susie a hermit? Because her continual nagging that "everyone else" has a TV in their bedroom finally wore down Mom and Dad. To assuage their guilt, they bought Susie her very own television. She no longer has to argue with the rest of the family over what shows to watch—she can go in her room and watch any show she wants!

In ***Bringing Learning Home,*** Mary Susan Miller cautions parents, "If you have not already succumbed, I urge you not to give your children their own television sets." A private TV invites isolation and lessens communication. If your child has his own television, strongly consider either removing it or setting strict limits on its use.

The rock star

Twelve-year-old Ricky turns every rectangular object into a mock electric guitar. His teacher is constantly annoyed by the soft drumbeat of two pencils on his desk.

It's pretty clear what program he watches on television between 3:00 and 5:00 while he waits for you to get home from work.

Don't blame Ricky for thinking MTV is the "coolest" thing to watch. It's fast-paced and glitzy—*designed* to lure Ricky and his cohorts. If it had been around when we were adolescents, we would have been hooked, too.

Before you decide how you feel about your son or daughter watching MTV, *you* need to watch it. Better yet, watch it with your child and discuss concerns that you have. Such a discussion will lend credibility to the limits you establish. If you are unable to be home to monitor your child's viewing, and have definitely decided you don't want your children watching MTV, you may wish to have your cable company scramble this station.

The cartoon consumer

The only things 6-year-old Timmy loves more than cartoons are the movable action figures of his cartoon heroes.

His mother, Debbie, faces the same dilemma every time she takes Timmy to the local discount store. If she indulges his desire for the latest character, she feels guilty for giving into his whims. Her busy schedule means that she and Timmy have limited time together, so disappointing him during their shopping trip also triggers guilt. Typically, Debbie gives in, then finds herself feeling angry a week later when Timmy has lost interest in the new toy he "had to have."

The American Academy of Pediatrics has blasted what they call "toy-based' programs," noting that in the past decade alone, some 70 toys were turned into programs that were little more than 30-minute commercials for the manufacturers.

The couch potato

Cindy is in the fifth grade, and her least favorite subject is Physical Education. She especially dreads the annual physical fitness tests—she can't do even part of a pull-up. Her mother is aware that Cindy needs to lose a few pounds, but she hasn't quite taken the initiative of ridding the house of high-calorie snack foods. She knows that Cindy watches TV and snacks every afternoon from 3:00 to 5:00, but "at least she's safe in the house."

A recent study conducted by the University of California at Irvine found that "watching two hours or more of TV daily turned out to be a stronger predictor of elevated cholesterol in children than any other factor looked at." Pediatricians found that "the kids who watched more TV tended to have more unhealthy dietary habits." In addition, these children tended to be more sedentary.

Such children often have a more difficult time concentrating in the classroom. If you have your own couch potato at home, and are unable to supervise his or her viewing, don't add to your guilt by having junk food available.

The fighter

On Monday, 7-year-old Jack is a soldier. On Tuesday, he's a Ninja warrior. On Wednesday, a policeman. His parents have bought him such elaborate dress-up accessories because they feel that role playing is healthy. Lately, though, they've begun to wonder about how far role playing should go—Jack has started continually imitating the aggressive action he sees on television. When Jack brings home a playground citation for fighting, his parents wonder if his role playing has finally gone too far.

Health magazine reports that "the American Academy of Pediatrics recently issued a strong warning about how television violence makes children more aggressive and prone to fighting." Many shows that children are naturally attracted to depict characters who solve their conflicts through violence rather than cooperation.

Younger children are particularly susceptible to TV violence. ***The National PTA Talks to Parents*** suggests that "if a show you decide to watch includes shootings or beatings, talk about the violence. Explain that violence is faked on TV, but be sure your child realizes that real guns can kill."

The patterns described above—the hermit, rock star, cartoon consumer, couch potato and fighter—can all be broken without doing away with your television set. It takes a relatively small amount of time to set up your own family limits for TV viewing. Once the limits are established, the time your children spend watching TV can be guilt-free productive time for you.

Resources for good viewing

Now that you have established limits on the amount of TV your children view, and considered the TV patterns you want them to avoid, it is time to make the TV they *do* watch as high quality as possible. Three simple ways to do this are to: get acquainted with your VCR, plan some of their viewing ahead of time, and familiarize yourself with quality shows and stations. Busy parents may hesitate to devote time to television in this manner, but doing so will buy you guilt-free time and make sure your children watch enriching shows.

"I can barely set the clock on my VCR!"

Most people who own VCRs don't know how to program them. They manage to set the clock, play movies that they rent, and perhaps record directly from the television. The problem is that when a quality show airs, busy parents are not usually standing idly by, waiting to press the "record" button. As a result, superior children's shows that could be taped for later viewing are never recorded.

The average VCR can store programming information about four different shows, allowing you to record these shows even when you are not home. It would probably take you less than thirty minutes with your manual to learn how to do this.

Learning how to make full use of your VCR enables you to develop a library of tapes without investing much money. *New York* magazine talks of today's kids "who walk around hugging their favorite videocassettes" much as earlier kids "clutched dog-eared books." A familiar and beloved tape can provide comfort to a tired child and peace to his busy mother or father.

"I don't have time to plan their shows!"

You don't have to. Let *them* do the planning at the kitchen table while you're making dinner. As they study the TV guide, they will be reading and practicing good decision-making skills. You will be close at hand to discuss and approve their choices. And if you make them write down the shows they plan to watch, they will be painlessly practicing more language-related skills.

It would be unrealistic to plan every single show in advance, but letting kids plan out some of their viewing makes them more discriminating. Since making a plan generates constructive talk about TV, kids begin to internalize their parent's likes and dislikes and develop their own.

An additional advantage to planned TV viewing is that it tends to make each program seem like a distinct event.

This makes it easier to turn the television off at the end of the program rather than leave it on as background noise.

"There aren't any good shows anyway!"

Actually, there are many innovative, high quality programs, especially on cable television. In a recent *Parents* magazine article, Bill Cosby explained that "if parents and children select programs wisely, TV can be an invaluable learning tool."

How do you find the enriching shows? Here are some hints:

- Ask friends who share your values what their kids watch.
- Flip through one of several books that rates kid's videos.
- Record or remember to watch any shows that focus on topics your child is studying at school. Make a note of any programs recommended by the teacher.
- Skim the children's section of your TV program guide and/or your cable guide.
- Familiarize yourself with the shows available on your local public television stations.
- If a show is done by the Children's Television Workshop, it's probably good. (They produce "Sesame Street" and many other award-winning shows).
- Nickelodeon has many good shows for children. Kids like them because they depict *real* kids, faults and all.

- Consider adding the Disney Channel, an outstanding source of quality movies and features to tape for your kids.
- The Arts & Entertainment cable station may be an alternative source of music exposure if you don't like MTV.

If you wisely use your TV and VCR, and steer your children in the direction of high quality shows, you will feel that TV is enriching rather than polluting their lives. The only way to make it even better is to watch good shows with the whole family!

Television as a family activity

At the end of a busy day, you want and need to spend time with your children. It would be nice to do an innovative art project or dash out to the children's library, but the reality is that you're often too exhausted to face a simple board game. On those nights, television can be the perfect family activity. What's more fun for a kid than munching popcorn in front of the TV, and watching a Disney movie *with Mom and Dad?*

In addition to relaxation, family viewing offers some other benefits:

1. Watching television together allows you to ***set a good example*** in terms of the kinds of shows you choose.
2. Family viewing enables you to ***discuss advertising***. Congress recently passed a bill limiting ads on children's programs to 12 minutes per hour during the week and 10 1/2 on weekends. Yale Professor Jerome Singer explains that "advertising

puts a great deal of pressure on children to buy everything from toys to snack foods." The *Journal of Nutrition* analyzed ads on 29 hours of children's TV and found that 82% were for edible items such as drinks and candy. By talking about ads, you can help your kids understand the real purpose of commercials.

3. Your presence also helps ***lessen the intensity*** of certain scenes. As our old friend Mr. Rogers says, "Children need to understand the difference between real and pretend—particularly on television where there is so much pretend that can be very scary." A TV show may spark a productive discussion that would not have come up otherwise.

When you watch TV as a family, you become more aware of the ways in which television affects your child. This knowledge helps you to place reasonable limits on the amount and quality of television that your child may watch.

As you incorporate these limits into the structure of your home life, your television will cease to be a "guilt box." Instead, it will become a source of both entertainment and education, an *asset* to your child's schooling rather than a liability.

Chapter Nine

Guilt-Free Checklist for Parents

"Parents must make room in their hearts and then in their houses and then in their schedules for their children... no parent is too busy."

— Jesse Jackson

It's true. **No parent is too busy.**

This is not to say that today's parents do not have hectic and complex schedules. We do. *You* do.

Nevertheless, one fact remains: Parents who are involved, concerned and supportive—*no matter how busy they are*—provide a critical link between their children and the educational process. Unnecessary guilt inhibits busy parents from making this connection as strong as it can be. By organizing and prioritizing, even the busiest parent can be more effectively involved.

This chapter is a summary of all the information sprinkled throughout the book, a checklist, if you will, for quick reference. There are seven sections with ten items in each.

As you read each list of ten, put a check by the activities that you do on a consistent basis. Some activities, such as reading with your child, should be done daily. Many of the school-related items (conferences, assisting with class activities, etc.) would obviously be done on a less frequent basis.

As you complete each category, add up the checks and write the total on the line provided. Transfer these totals to the chart on page 151 to get a clear picture of *your* current educational involvement. (We'll tell you how to interpret your graph at the end of this summary.)

Home structure

- ❑ Organize your child's room
- ❑ Have your child keep his room clean
- ❑ Assign one specific chore
- ❑ Eliminate one negative behavior by being consistent
- ❑ Reinforce one positive behavior
- ❑ Eat dinner as a family three times per week
- ❑ Fix at least four well-balanced dinners each week
- ❑ Choose fast food that is low in fat
- ❑ Set a consistent bedtime
- ❑ Establish a sleep routine

Total items checked: ___________

Home communication

- ❑ Believe your child is capable
- ❑ Praise your child for his or her effort
- ❑ Do not accept inappropriate behavior

- ❑ Do accept your child's feelings
- ❑ Express your feelings using "I" statements
- ❑ Look your kids in the eye when you speak
- ❑ Ask for opinions and listen to answers
- ❑ Stop what you are doing and "listen"
- ❑ Send a positive nonverbal message
- ❑ Use a negative nonverbal cue

Total items checked: ___________

School involvement

- ❑ Send supplies to school for a special project
- ❑ Provide food for a party
- ❑ Volunteer in the classroom
- ❑ Speak positively about school and your child's teacher
- ❑ Attend a school function (carnival, science fair, etc.)
- ❑ Show interest in your child's work
- ❑ Talk to your child about school events
- ❑ Read the school newsletter
- ❑ Assist the PTA in some manner
- ❑ Learn to say "no" when appropriate

Total items checked: ___________

School communication

- ❑ Get a list of the staff at your child's school
- ❑ Ask for a list of the school district administrators
- ❑ Attend any scheduled parent conferences
- ❑ Go to Back-to-School Night
- ❑ Read and discuss class newsletters or progress reports

- ❑ Attend Open House
- ❑ Communicate major concerns to your child's teacher
- ❑ Write your child's teacher a note of appreciation
- ❑ Praise your child's good grades
- ❑ Make a plan to raise poor grades

Total items checked: ___________

Reinforcing academics

- ❑ Read to or with your child
- ❑ Establish a homework routine
- ❑ Assist in organizing and understanding assignments
- ❑ Go over completed work
- ❑ Compliment your child for work well done
- ❑ Spend five minutes discussing the school day
- ❑ Play a game of some sort with your child
- ❑ Write your child a note and have him answer it
- ❑ Hang up your child's work
- ❑ Know what's being studied in the classroom and discuss it

Total items checked: ___________

Extracurricular activities

- ❑ Become aware of your child's interests
- ❑ Sign up for one structured extracurricular activity
- ❑ Help your child meet a friend through an outside activity
- ❑ Encourage your child's efforts in an athletic area
- ❑ Expose your child to an aspect of the arts
- ❑ Help your child become aware of other cultures

- ❑ Be sure that your child has adequate free time
- ❑ Encourage active outdoor play
- ❑ Do something active with your child weekly
- ❑ Watch for signs of fatigue or burnout

Total items checked: ___________

Television

- ❑ Limit TV viewing to one hour on school days
- ❑ Turn the TV off if no one is watching it
- ❑ Help your child plan out TV shows for the next week
- ❑ Keep the TV off during meals
- ❑ Watch a family movie with your children
- ❑ Avoid TV during homework time
- ❑ Discuss TV violence with your children
- ❑ Encourage your children to watch public television
- ❑ Talk about TV advertising
- ❑ Become aware of high quality children's shows and movies

Total items checked: ___________

Filling in your chart

Take the seven numbers you have written in and transfer them as dots to the appropriate squares in the chart on page 151.

(We've already marked it with sample scores for parents doing reasonably well...except in the areas of school involvement and television.)

If *your* dots consistently fall below the half-way mark —scores of 4 or less—you may want to refer back to the chapter that covers that topic and reread it.

How Are You Doing?

	Home Structure	Communication	School Involvement	School Communication	Reinforce Academics	Extra Curricular Activities	Television
10							
9						●	
8					●		
7	●			●			
6							
5		●					
4			●				●
3							
2							
1							

If most of your dots are in the upper half of this chart, you are taking a proactive role in your child's education. You need not feel guilty about your busy schedule, because you are already an effective partner in your child's learning.

In the 1980's, many people tried to become "super parents"...and most failed. Most people just *can't* "do it all." And *you shouldn't feel you have to,* especially after reading this book.

Laura Ziskin, a prominent Hollywood producer, described a typical conversation with her friends Sally Field and Goldie Hawn to *People* magazine. "All we talk about together is how we're dealing with our work and our children...I learned I was only one person and could only do what I could do. The net result was I began to look at my compromises as positive rather than negative."

We are all concerned about helping our children be successful and productive. Therefore, whether you are a movie star, a grocery clerk, an accountant, a flight attendant, a homemaker, a business woman or a working father, balancing your time and assisting your children should be your number one priority. Following the steps outlined in this book, you will erase unnecessary guilt, make the home/school partnership as effective as it can be, and provide your children with the support they need on their educational journey.

We hope you do as much as *you* can—guilt-free!

Bibliography

Erasing The Guilt

Black, Ginger E., Making The Grade, New York: Carole Publishing Group, 1989.

Bombeck, Erma, "Motherhood is Running on Guilt," *The Daily Sun/Post*, October 8, 1990.

Canter, Lee and Canter, Marlene, Assertive Discipline For Parents, New York: Harper & Row, 1988.

Canter, Lee and Hausner, Lee, Homework Without Tears, New York: Harper & Row, 1987.

Croft, Doreen J., Parents And Teachers: A Resource Book For Home, School, And Community Relations, California: Wadsworth Publishing Company, 1979.

Cutright, Melitta J., The National PTA Talks To Parents, New York: Doubleday, 1989.

Dietz, William Jr. M.D., "Kids & TV, Just How Healthy a Relationship Is It?," *NEA Today*, Dec. 1988, p 9.

Dreikurs, Rudolf, M.D., and Soltz, Vicki, Children: The Challenge, New York: E.P. Dutton, 1987.

Educational Leadership, Issue devoted to Parent Involvement, October, 1989.

Elmer - Dewitt, Philip, "The Great Experiment," *Time*, Fall, 1990, p 72 - 75.

Fields, Terri, Help Your Child Make The Most Out Of School, New York: Villard Books, 1987.

Finkelstein, Alix, Editor, "Curb on Kids' TV Ads", *Parents Magazine*, March, 1991, p 15.

Friedman, Sara Ann, How Was School Today, Dear?, New York: Readers Digest, 1977.

Fulghum, Robert, All I Really Needed To Know I Learned In Kindergarten, New York: Ballantine Books, 1988.

Goldman, Judy O'Brien, "The Taming of the Tube," *Health*, July/August, 1990, p 42-43.

Hopper, Chris, The Sports-Confident Child, New York: Random House, Inc., 1988.

Knezevich, Stephen J., Administration of Public Education, New York: Harper & Row, 1975.

Lindgren, Kristina, "UCI Study Links Kids' TV Habits, Higher Cholesterol," *Los Angeles Times*, November 13, 1990.

Losen, Stuart M. and Diament, Bert, Parent Conferences In The Schools, Massachusetts: Allyn and Bacon Inc., 1978.

Miller, Mary Susan, Bringing Learning Home, New York: Harper & Row, 1981.

NEA Today Staff, "Sensible TV Viewing Goes with Better Reading," *NEA Today*, December, 1988, p 34.

Nelson, Pamela A., "How to Make Schools and Parents Partners," *The Education Digest*, September, 1988, p 38 - 40.

Newsweek—Special Edition on Education, *Newsweek*, Fall/Winter, 1990 - 1991.

Prevention Staff, "TV Perils," *Prevention*, June 1988, p 8-9.

Pryor, Kelli, "Videos For the Kideos," *New York*, June 6, 1988, p 35.

Rasinski, Timothy, and Fredericks, Anthony D., "Can Parents Make a Difference?," *The Reading Teacher*, October, 1989, p 84 - 85.

Rich, Dorothy, "Activities to Strengthen Reading at Home," *Instructor*, October, 1988, P 41 - 49.

Rogers, Fred, "What Kids Should Believe About Make-Believe," *The Cable Guide*, October, 1990, p 44.

Rosemond, John K., Ending The Homework Hassle, New York: Andrews and McMeel, 1990.

Samuels, Mike, M.D. and Nancy, The Well Child Book, New York: Simon & Schuster, 1982.

Sipchen, Bob, "Tuning In the Spirit," *Los Angeles Times*, November 22, 1990.

Smith, Lynn, "School Uses Touch Tone to Reach Out to Parents," *Los Angeles Times*, November 12, 1990.

Stainback, William and Susan, How To Help Your Child Succeed In School, Minnesota: Meadowbrook Press, 1988.

Index

Erasing The Guilt